Plum Point Folio

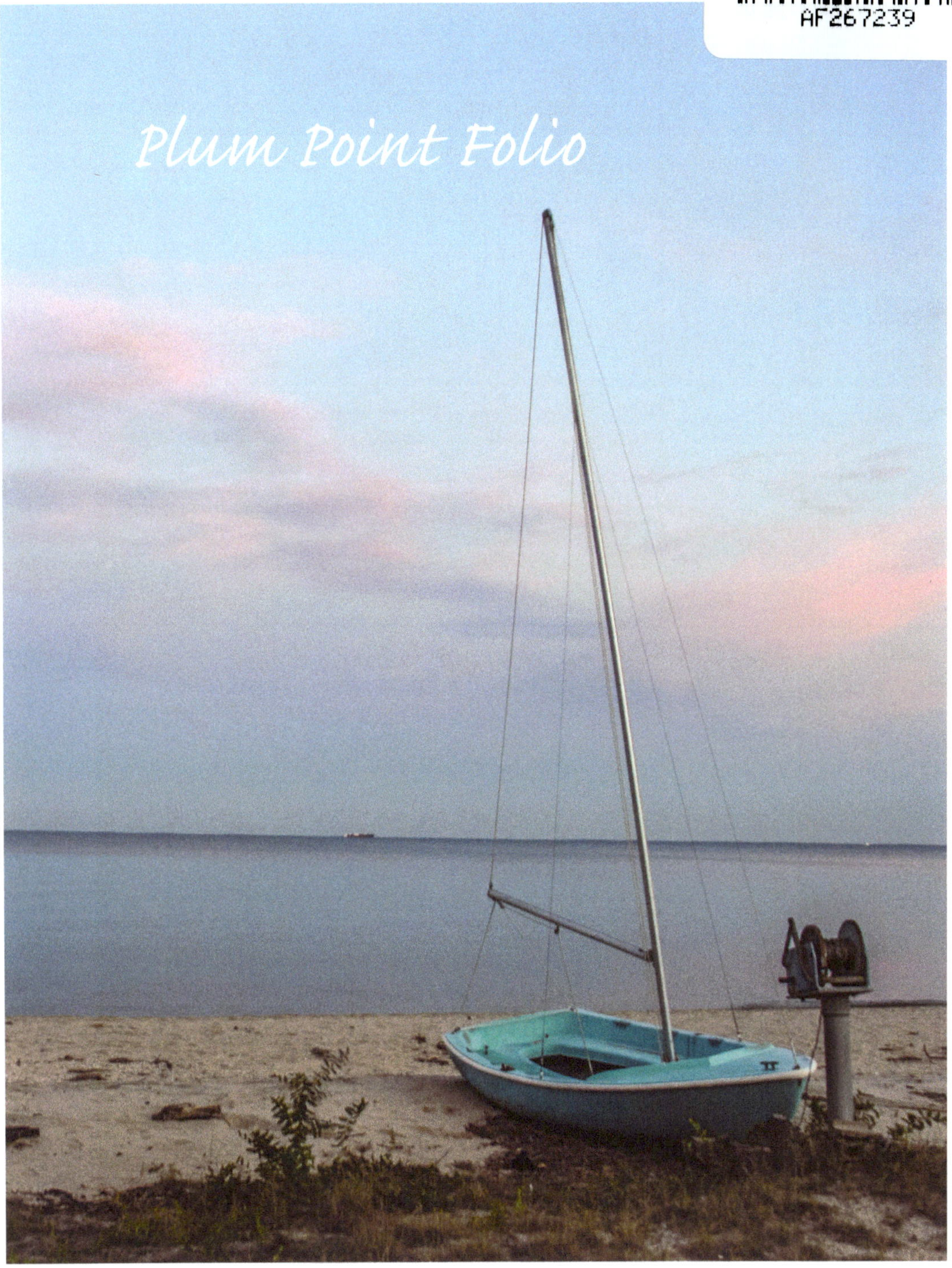

Poems by Christine Higgins

Photographs by Kevin Higgins

10% of the proceeds from the sale of this book go to
The Chesapeake Bay Foundation

Copyright @ 2016 by Christine Higgins

Author: Christine Higgins
Photography: Kevin Higgins
Book design and layout: Suzanne Shelden

ISBN: 978-0-9975649-0-7

First Edition
2016

Published by Shelden Studios
Prince Frederick, Maryland
www.sheldenstudios.com

To order a custom framed photograph from this book visit
www.kevinhigginsphotography.com

to learn more about this book, other writings by the author, and events, visit
www.christinehigginswriter.com

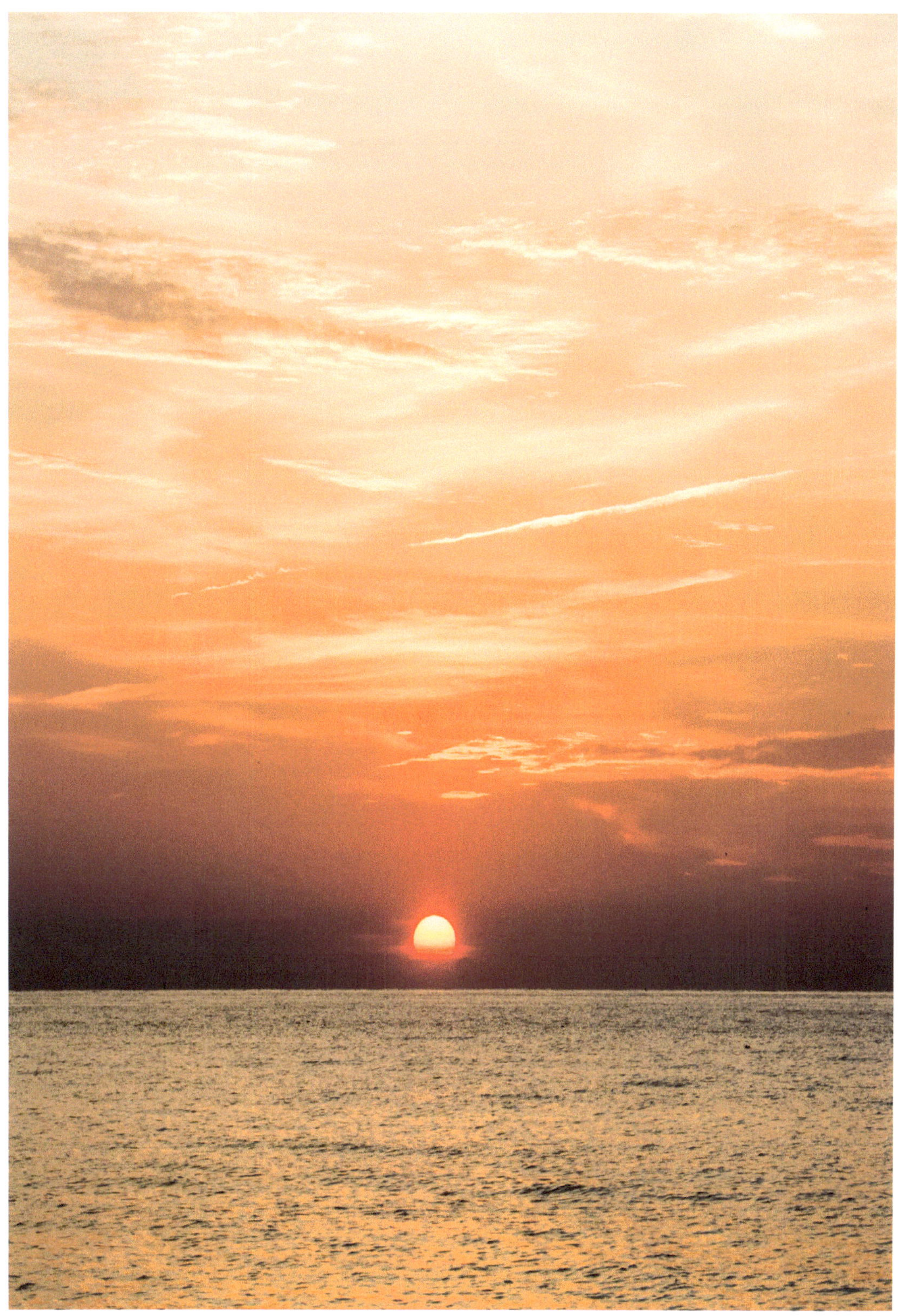

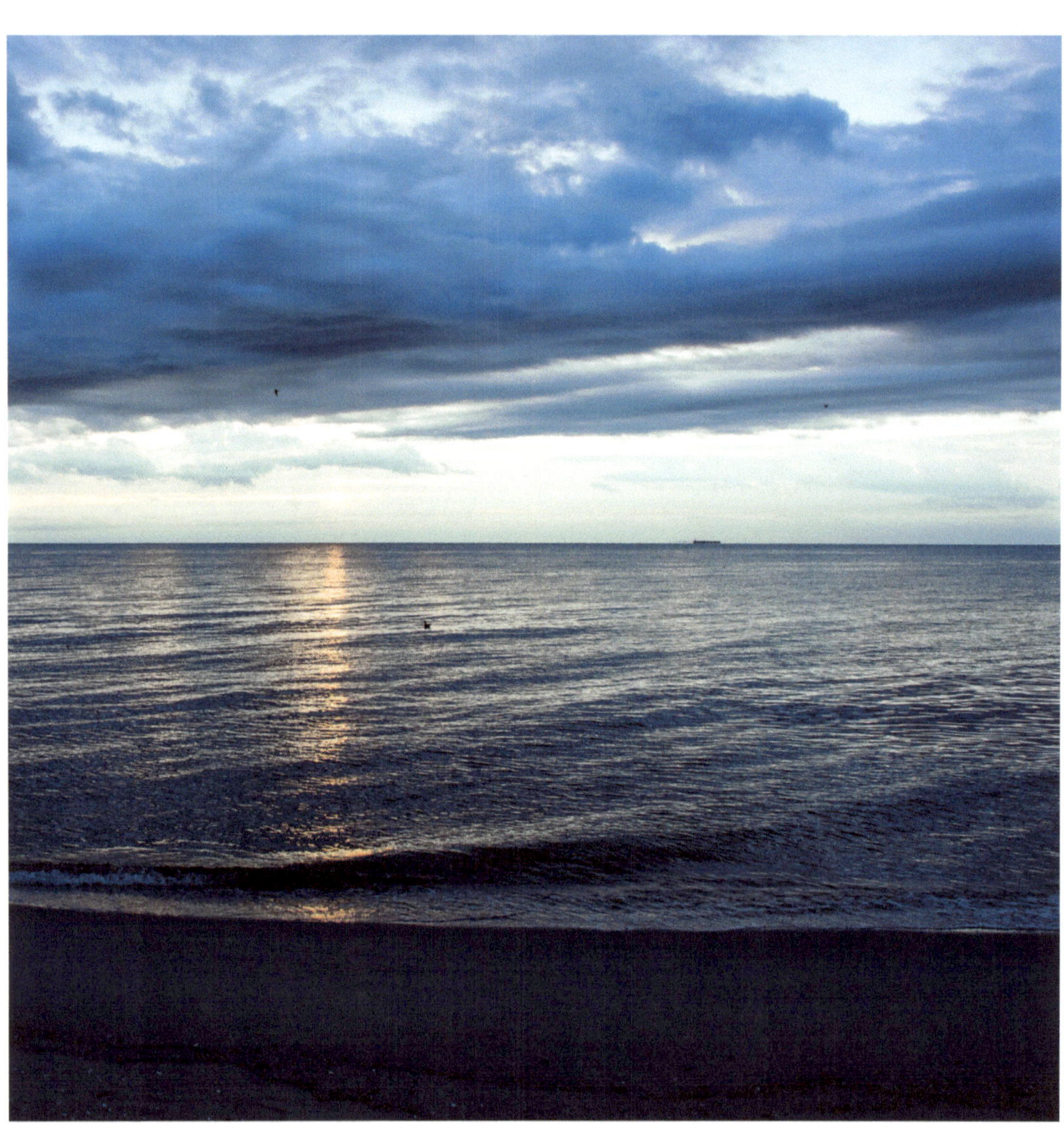

Plum Point Folio

poetry by
Christine Higgins

photography by
Kevin Higgins

June 2016

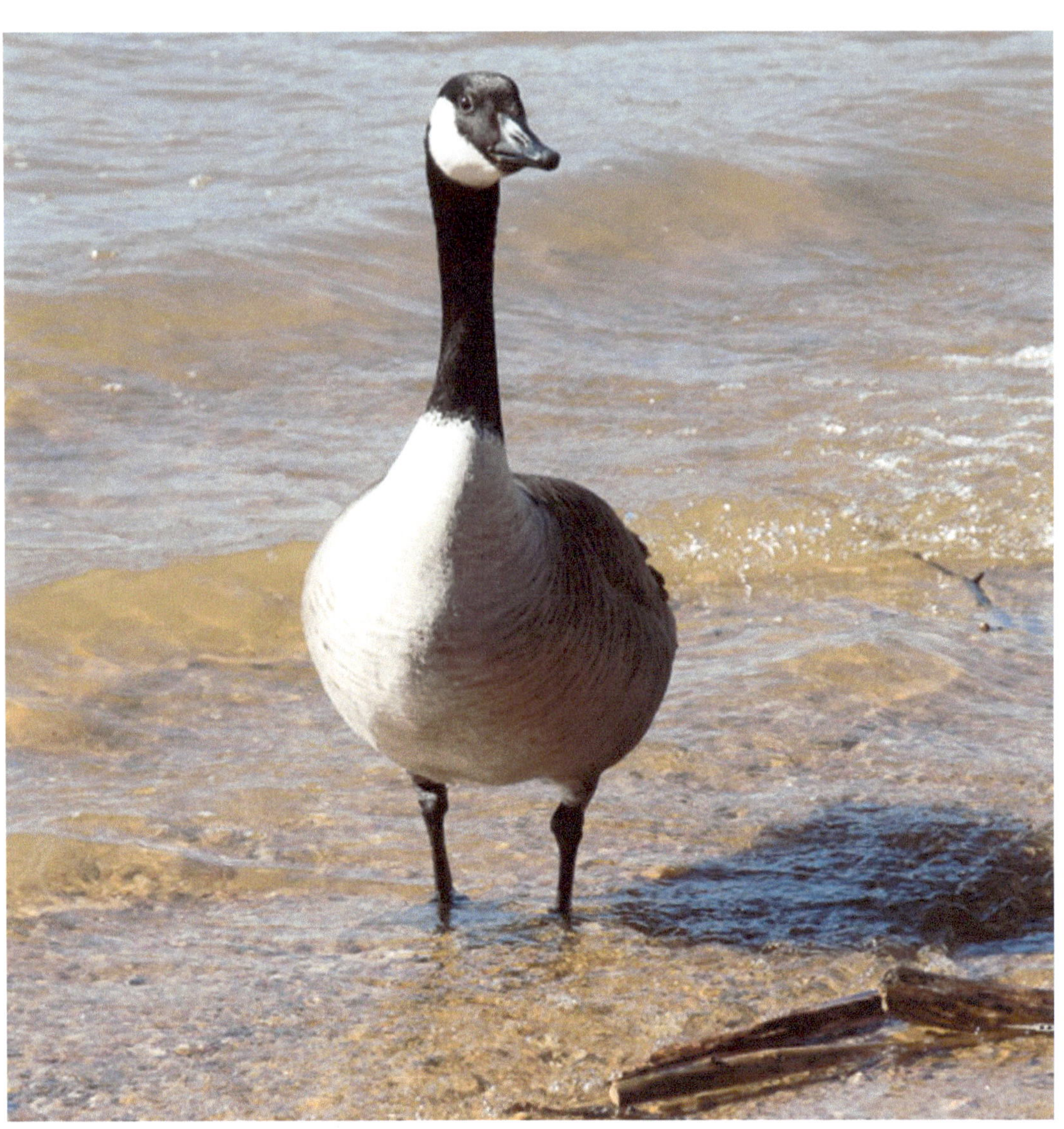

Contents

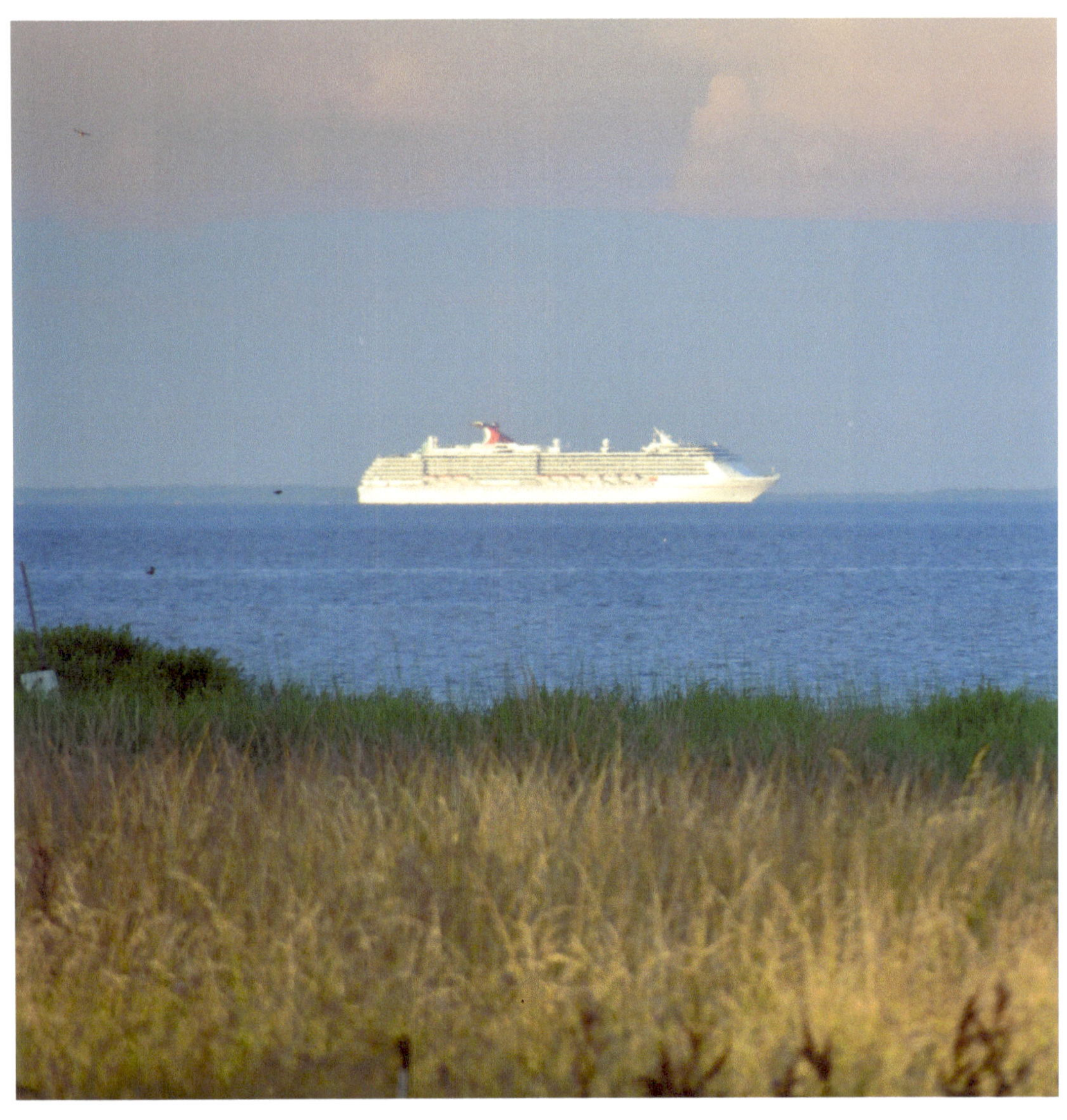

Notes on Plum Point

"Heaven and earth never agreed better to frame a place for man's habitation."
Captain John Smith, 1607

Brown bottle beer glass,
the lesser greens & blues,
sometimes a whole neck rubbed smooth,
cornelian colored stones
glistening in wet sand.
The ever-changing clouds,
a mixture of baby blue and white cotton,
landscapes painterly in the making.

Our only task:
sit in beach chairs
and watch the moving screen
from our fixed state—
sailboats, ocean liners, catamarans.

Man or woman
has no need for book or magazine,
headphones or laptop.
Just absorb this gift:
the calm upon the water
the sun's stimulating glitter,
how it heightens
our desire to be at one.

Old Black and White

You can pinpoint the time
pretty well, thanks to the skinny
man in striped bathing suit
down to his knees.
Friends gathered on the grass—
three seated, two standing
under the shade of a tree.
One woman wears a long skirt.
Each one holds an ice-cream cone.
Perhaps they got them at the
Plum Point store—the one
you hear about but is no more.

Look closely and you can see
they're listening to music
from a portable record player.
Swimmers and splashing children
fill in the background.
I like to think this tableau
is a Sunday—a day of rest,
a day of leisure I could capture
with a brush and paints,
my own déjeuner sur l'herbe.
That's still here—these many
years later—cerulean blue,
the puffy white clouds, the trees
a deep shade of ultramarine.

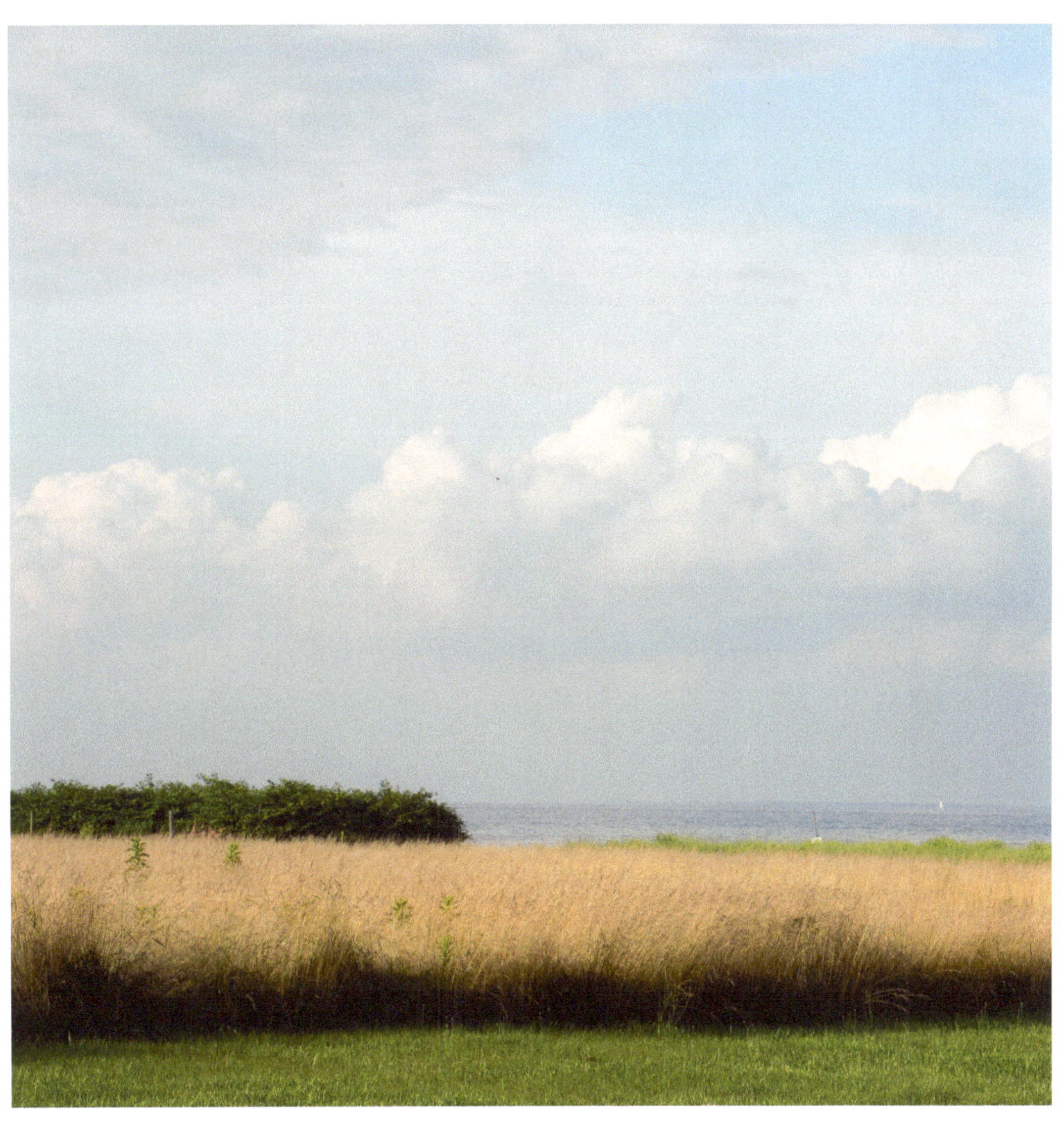

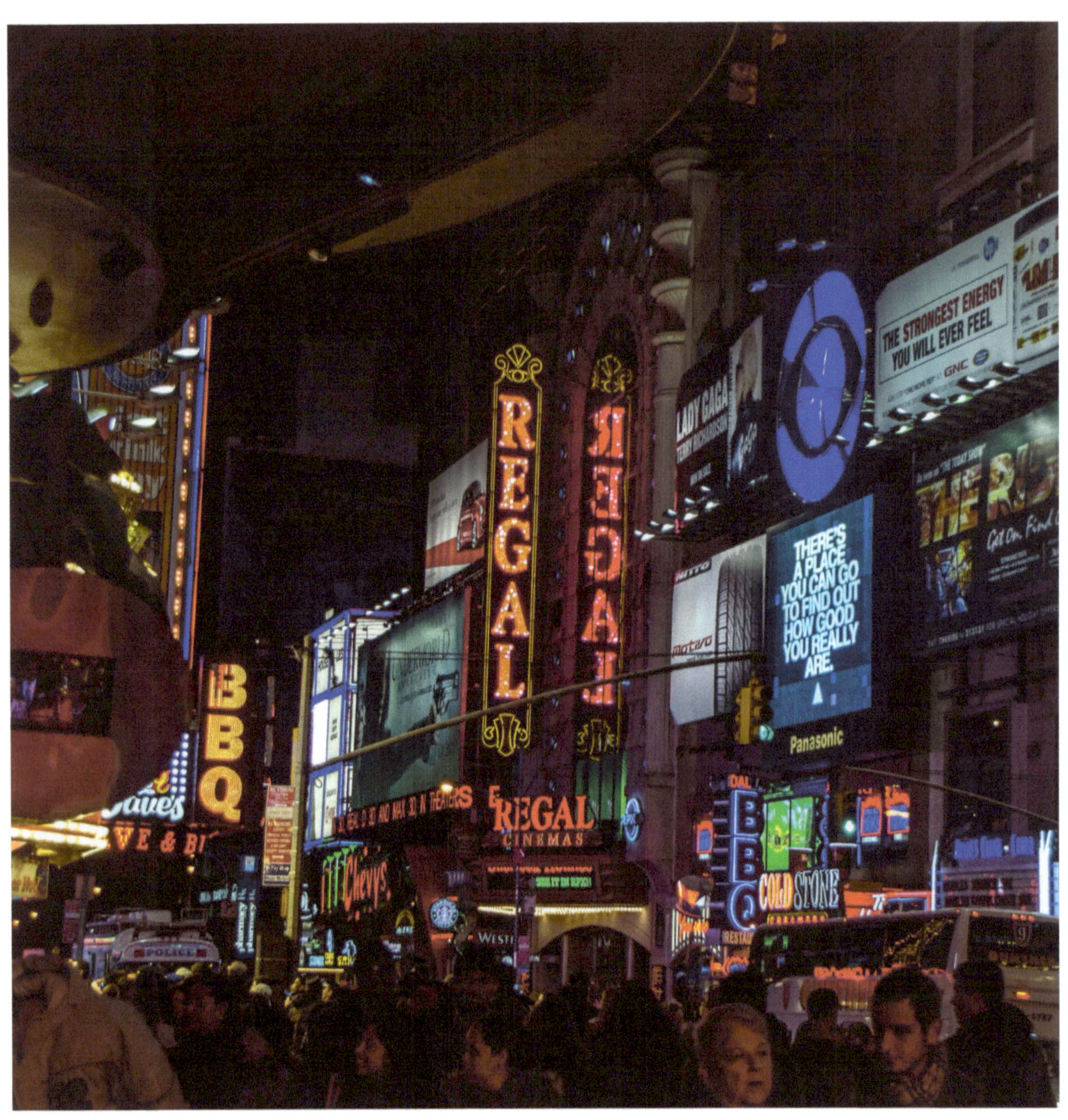

REGAL
REGAL
REGAL
CINEMAS
BBQ
Dave's
VE & BI
Chevys
BBQ
COLD STONE
THE STRONGEST ENERGY
YOU WILL EVER FEEL
GNC
LADY GAGA
TERRY RICHARDSON
THERE'S
A PLACE
YOU CAN GO
TO FIND OUT
HOW GOOD
YOU REALLY
ARE.
Panasonic
POLICE
WESTE

Natural Habitat

1. New York

I learned how to squeeze
myself into a rush hour subway car
how to maneuver throngs of people on Fifth Avenue
without so much as grazing another shoulder,
how to order my morning take-out
when the counter lady hollered, "Next!"
I knew how to step off the curb and hail a cab.
I loved the museums, the big name
department stores, the famous buildings.
I walked everywhere,
drank in the riotous colors—
orange umbrellas, red flowers in buckets,
yellow taxis, hot pink and cool blue neon.

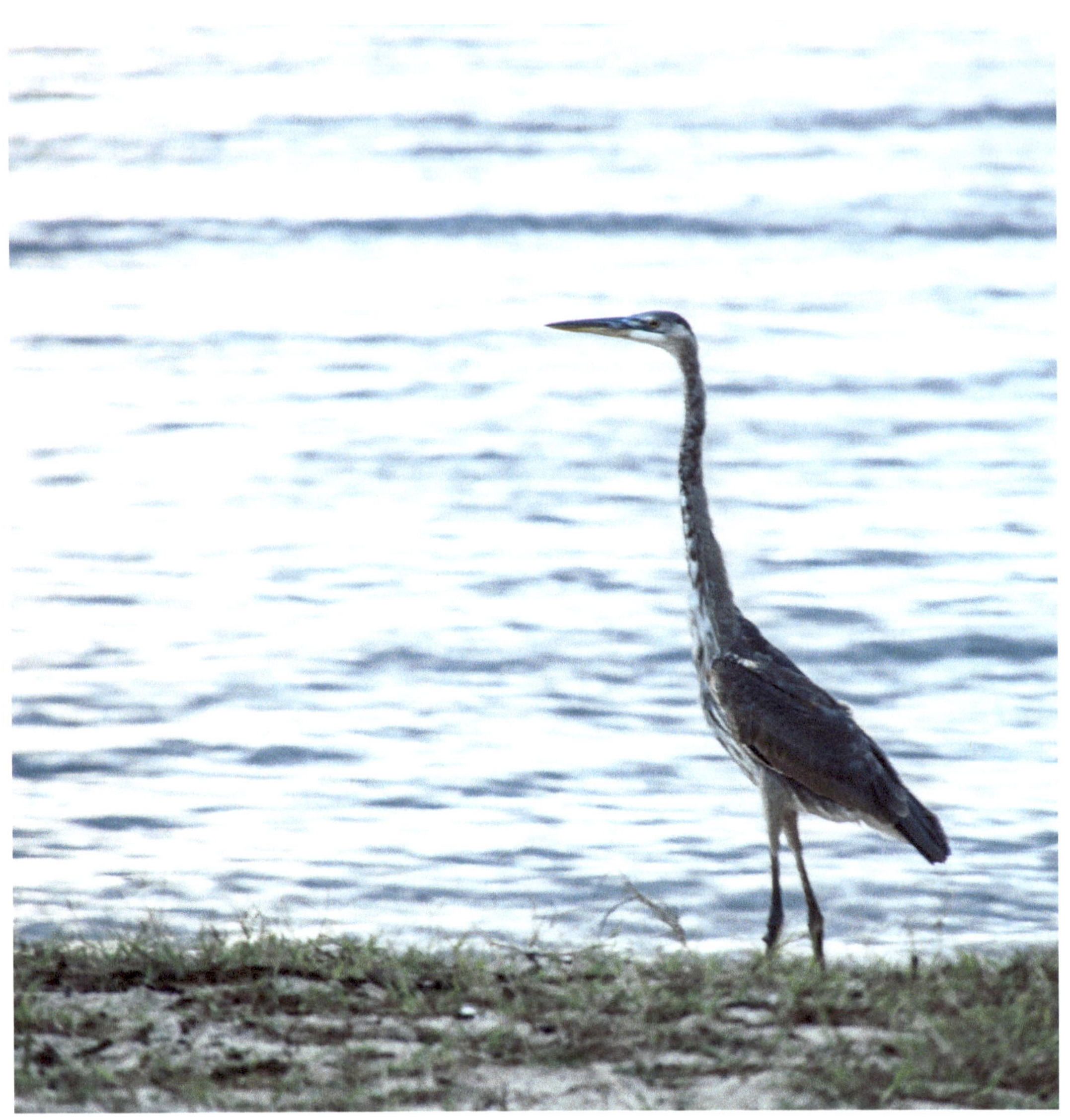

2. The Chesapeake Bay

My life is taken up
with walking the shoreline,
picking up remnants of ship iron,
sharks' teeth and beach glass.
I've learned the sting ray and the skate
are both in the Batoid family,
but have different kinds of teeth.
Near Calvert Cliffs, I search for fossils
made when the sea level
fell and rose over 10 million years.
I watch the heron drop his legs
behind him like a dancer
as he flies out over the water.
When the sun sets, it casts
a pink spell
on the slow-moving tankers.

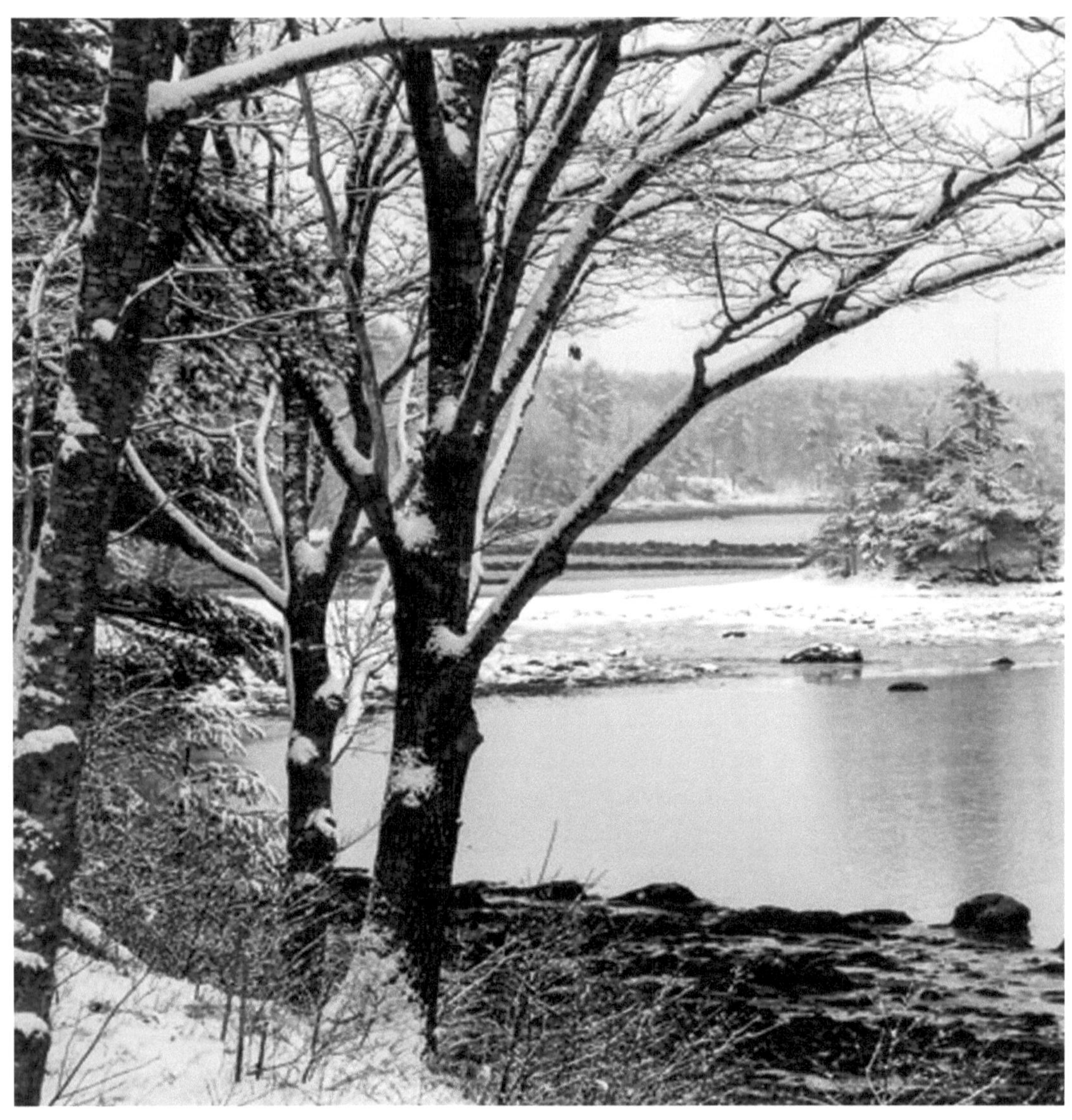

Snow

A severe storm sweeps along the East Coast.
Here in Baltimore, the backyard pines
bow down with the weight of ice.
Cars disappear under mountains of white.
Miles away in New York, they are preparing
for my grandmother's funeral.

My grandmother cared for me when I was a child.
Together we did the forbidden things:
watched TV in the daytime, read comic books,
ate orange ice pops and graham crackers
slathered with butter.

The only time I ever saw her cry
was when her old and blind mother died from cancer.
We were all assembled to say good-bye,
and I saw my grandmother gripping the edge
of the casket, willing it not to close.
I saw the pallbearer pry her fingers away.

The weatherman says twenty-two inches
have already fallen. Snow is gathering
around the house, like drifts of cotton batting,
as if it might soften the terrible truth:
It's here that I need to let her go.

Another Year Turning

Crackling cold night
when the white
disc of a moon
shines on the water
shines on the trees' branches
sheathed in ice.

I am a woman
in a sewing shop
searching for lace
to decorate the tree.
I find ornaments
of silvered glass,
boxes of real tinsel.
They are all mine already.
I am reminded of old friends,
getting older.

Another year turns.
Long white icicles
pierce the black night.

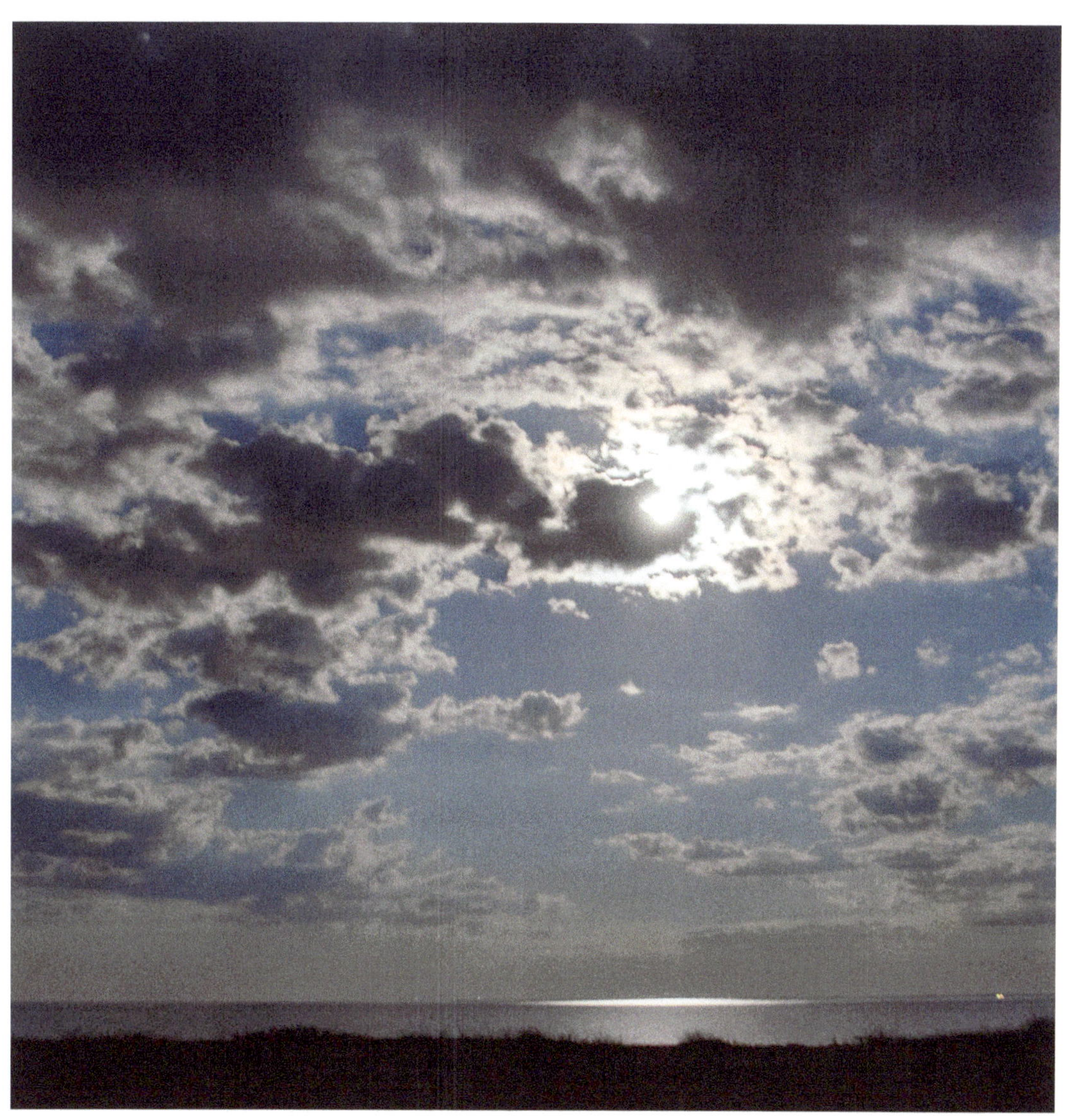

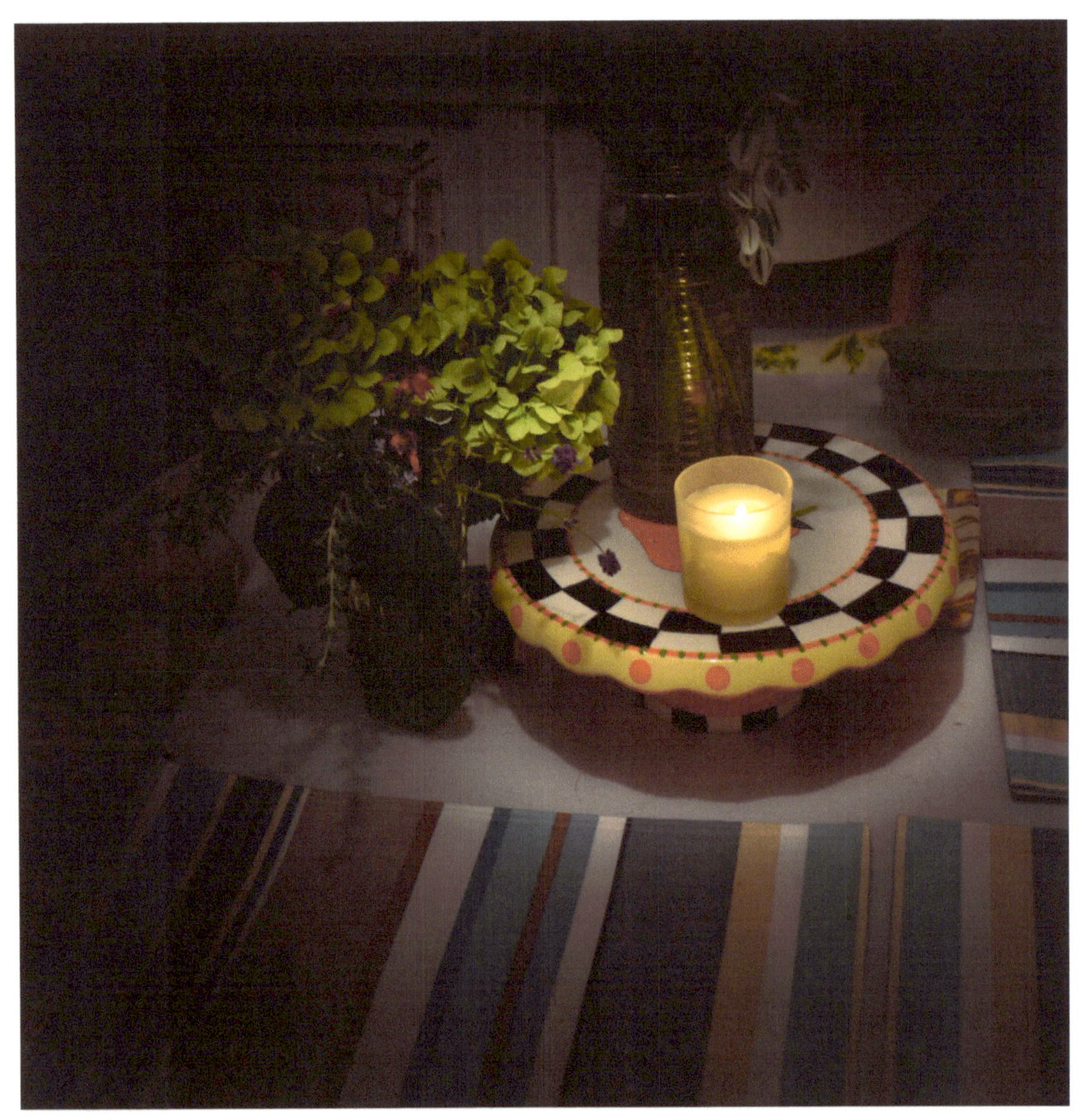

A Hard Rain

So hard, the water slides
down the window panes.
The wind, so persistent,
a whooshing sound—
not rising and falling
but thrumming from the constant
shake of the tree limbs.
The sky is pale, blanched white,
above a gun metal bay.
The white caps roll in,
the waves thrash the shore.

I like watching the elements
at work with such intensity—
akin to my own desires.
Still, I feel safe here in this little house,
protected from sorrow, comforted
by the idea of what endures.

I want to plumb the depths
of why I'm here, I want to say:
I promise to carry on.
I'm not afraid.

Reprise

Lilacs surround the herb garden,
drape the white roof
of a red house, line the path
I walk every morning.

In the city, I bought lilacs,
lifted them dripping
from a yellow pail
outside the Korean grocery.

Here, they grow on multiple branches,
I watch them fade from dark
to colored buds with little crosses
that open into pale blue flowers.

The fiddlehead ferns sway.
I see how much more they have let
their heads uncurl in green.

Each frond dips like a dancer.
Everything changes as fast as it changes.

Today, rain has left droplets
on the baby pines, and drenched
the heads of the lilacs.

I think their loveliness is gone,
but then a sudden heat
carries their fragrance again.

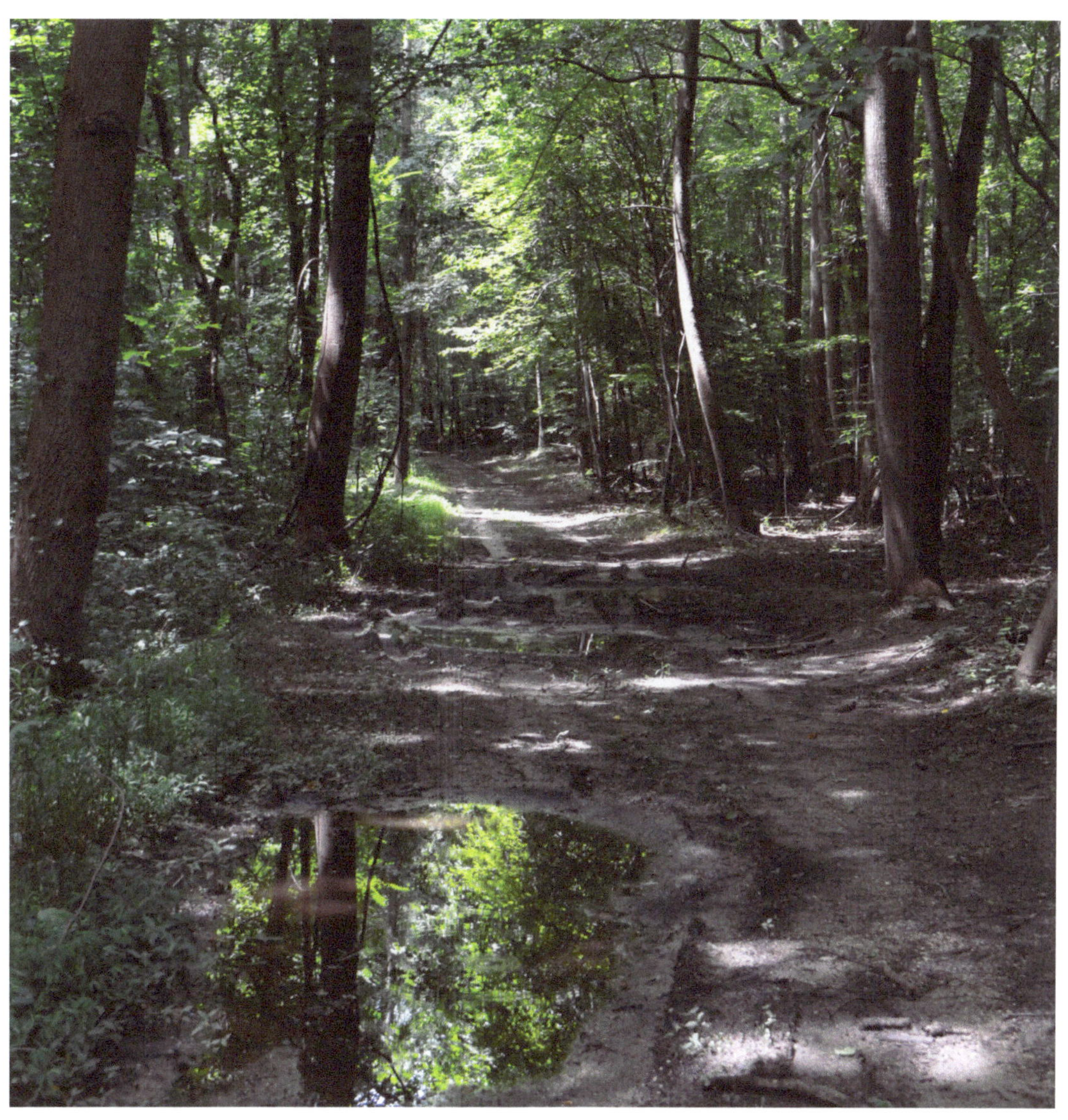

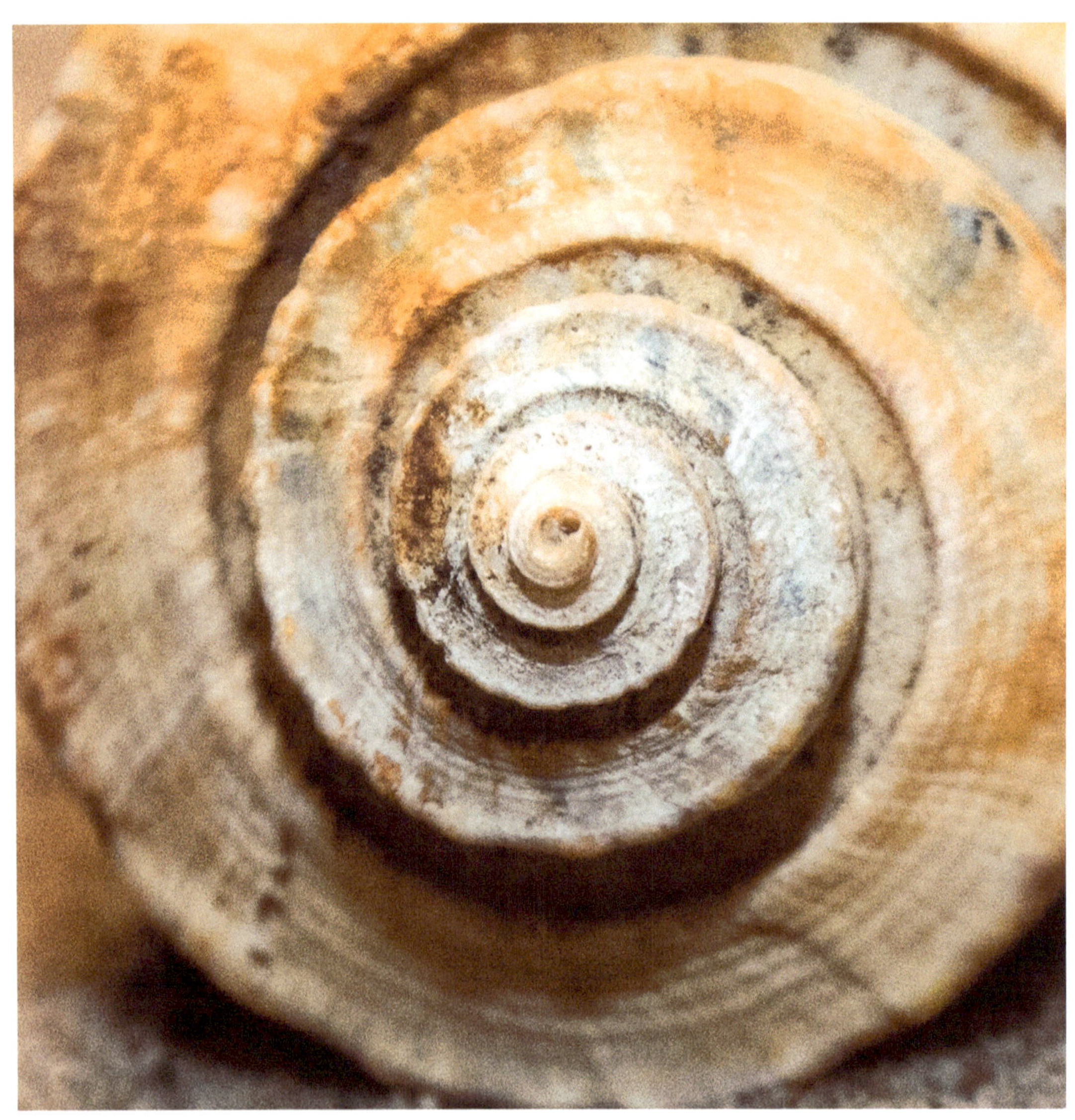

Knobbed Whelk

inside:
peach satin color
my grandmother's bed jacket

outside:
faded colors of summer
bleached grey and white and tan

resting here
on the sand:
well defined spines and
knobs made by the turning
of the segmented snail

solitary work: creating
whorls on an axis
an ancient vessel
a world unto itself

Beach Glass

Not mined gems
like rubies or diamonds
but gems nonetheless
made by what is left behind
as trash, rubbed by sand,
refined by waves and currents.

I've trained my eye
to find the emerald green
or amber brown of beer bottles.
Rarer, the cobalt blue
of Vaseline jars, or the milky
white of medicine bottles.
Relics, now that everything
is sold in plastic.

Older pieces, tossed
into slivers, icicles, smoothed shards--
aqua blue and olive green,
small enough to call them
mermaid's tears.
Treasured—those pieces
without shiny spots, well-frosted.

The best surprise—
a whole bottle neck
or only the curve of one,
harmless now that it's been
tumbled by the sea,
or the thick bases
bearing secret messages:
raised numbers, brand names:
Duraglass.

A lovely meditation
as I walk the shoreline.
Then the joy to see them later
collected in a candy dish,
nested together.

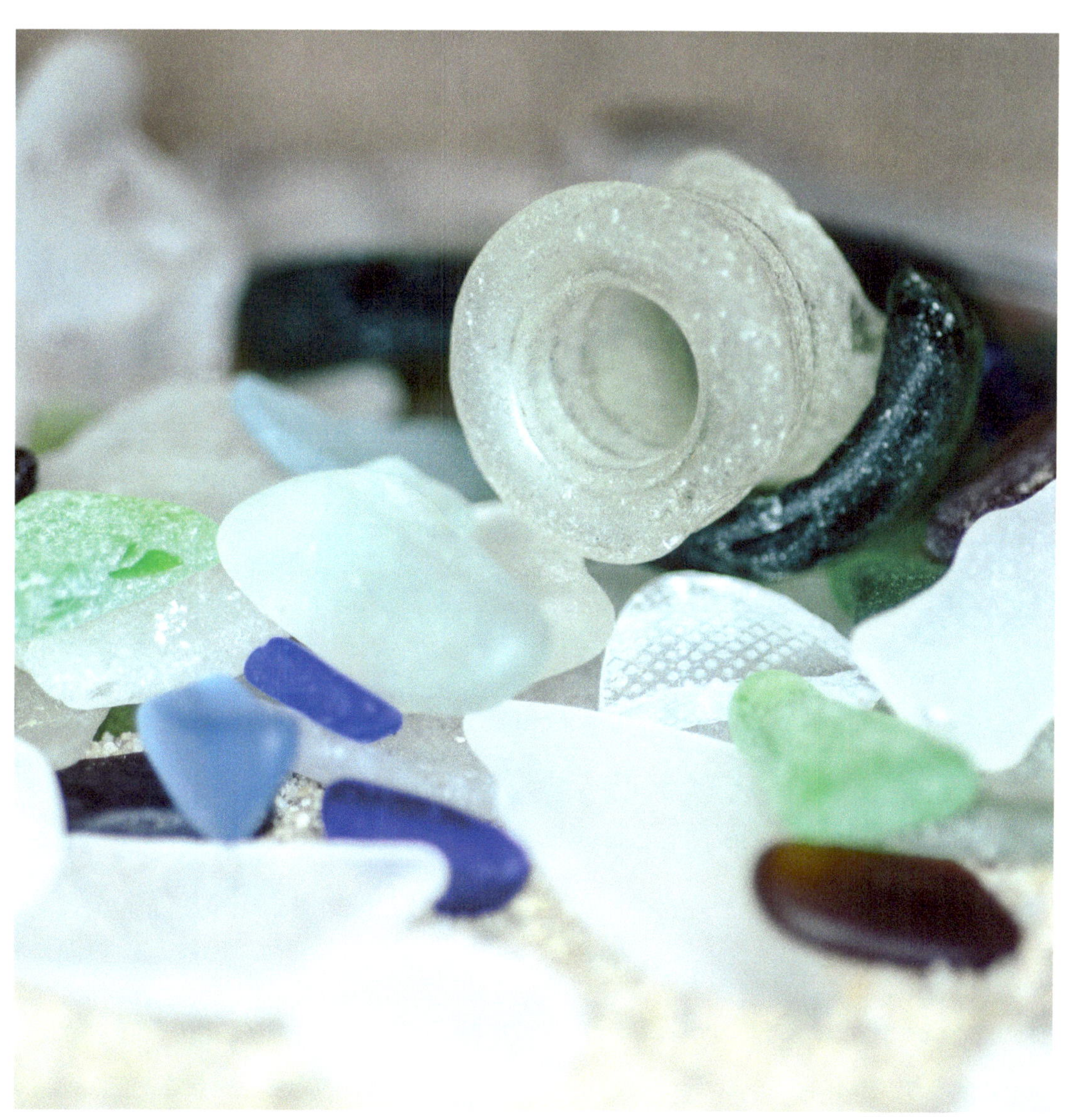

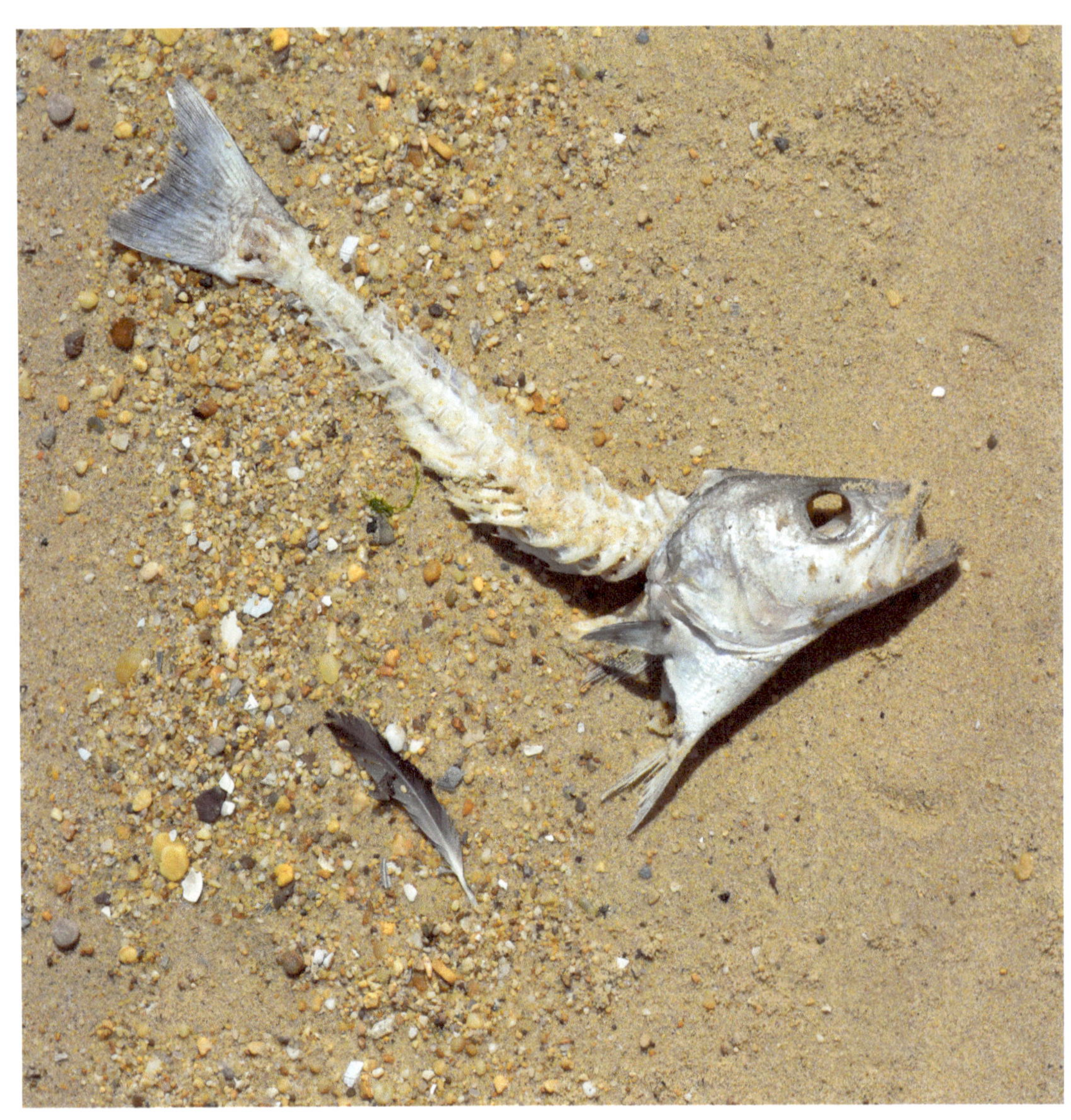

Bay Shoreline

moon jellies
   washed ashore

clear beach glass
   hardly any green

light blue tampon holder
clam shell bits
Doritos bag

rockfish—
   mouth agape
   and frozen stare

shiny bits of brown stones
   first appearing
   as treasured shark's teeth

blown dry grasses
bleached driftwood
skinny crab legs

red-beaked turkey vulture
   consummate scavenger

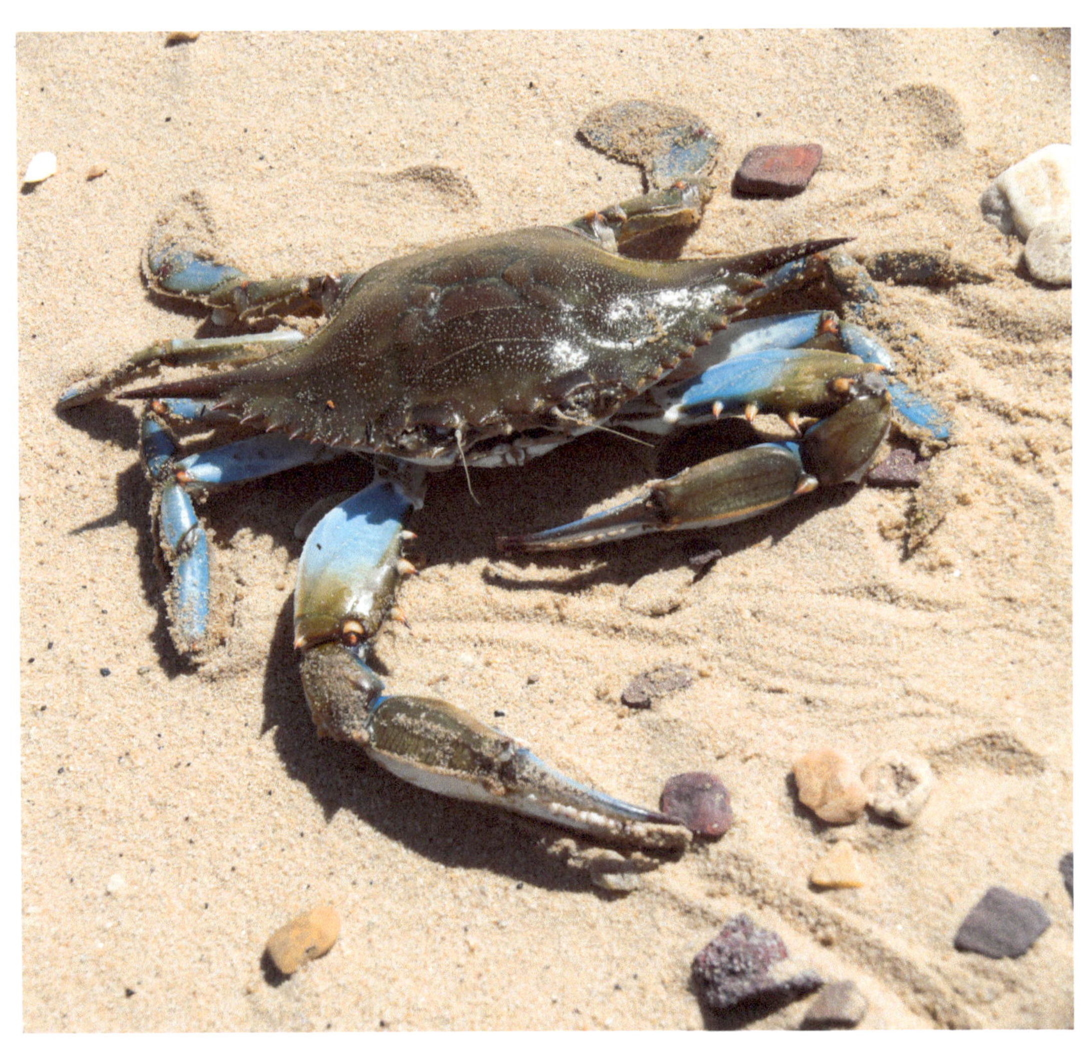

Chesapeake Crab

I marvel at the blue crab
crossing the sand in a stately gait,
no hurry, or so he thinks.
He's moving down the beach,
hauling his verdi gris shell
with his six startling legs of turquoise blue.
The front pincers—for plucking snails
from their shells—are tipped bright red
like new rust. They carry him
back to the water, to his home in the grasses.

All the articulated legs are jointed
like fine jewelry, polished
then washed with a brush stroke of blue.
Last to disappear are his back appendages
shaped at the ends like pumpkin seeds,
filmy white, mother of pearl.

He shines in the morning sun
that rises over the Chesapeake,
where he still reigns as king.

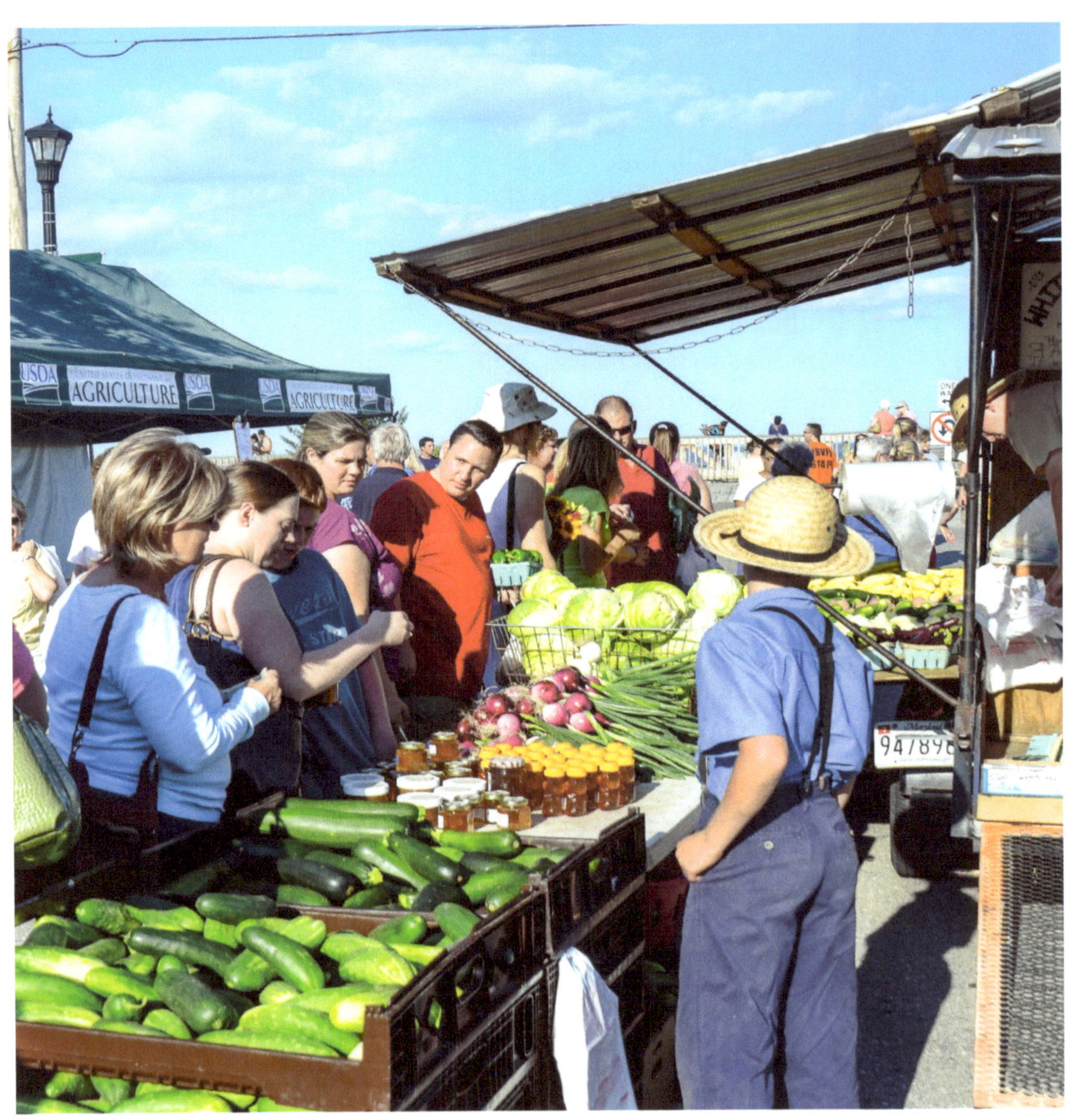
USDA
UNITED STATES DEPARTMENT OF
AGRICULTURE
USDA
AGRICULTURE
947896

Let's Get Some Crabs

I'm not from these parts,
so I had to learn it back then,
when I was newly married—
this particular delight in mounds
of crabs, scalded red and crusted in
Old Bay, dumped onto brown paper
covering any old table.

Our friends and neighbors hoisted
their wooden mallets, ready to strike.
It seemed to me the battle
had already been fought.
Those poor fellows looked up
with beady black eyes, their pincers
no longer moving—defeated.

My new husband taught me how
to pick a crab—turn it over, pull
back the apron, dig out the mustard
with your pinky finger. I learned
to twist the bigger legs into flowers
of luscious meat, moist and flavorful.
Still, not much yield, I thought,
for so much work.

My husband and his friends
sat for hours—picking, sipping beer,
talking. They never got up
from the table. Like a meditation.

I've been here long enough now
to see it's about the gathering,
a ritual that strikes the heart
maybe more than the palette,
the coming together over a couple
dozen crabs, talk that's never heavy—
about the weather, small changes.
Enjoying the fruits of their labor.

An Excellent Walk

with Cooper,
my four legged companion.
Today, longer than usual,
almost down to the darker green
and the sandy brown cliffs.
Head down, looking for beach glass,
I'm fooled over and over
by the bits of green
that turn out to be leaves.
I find three chunks,
larger than usual—
two white, one brown.

Down by the white cottages
we meet a black Lab.
And after a bout of tail wagging,
the Lab hops in the row boat
with his master, and adopts
a regal pose in the prow.
We watch them swing out into the bay
under a picture perfect sky.
On our way back home
we're careful not to step
on honey bees in the clover.

Sitting on the porch, I discover
the one brown glass shard
is a treasure
with raised letters that spell
REFIL.

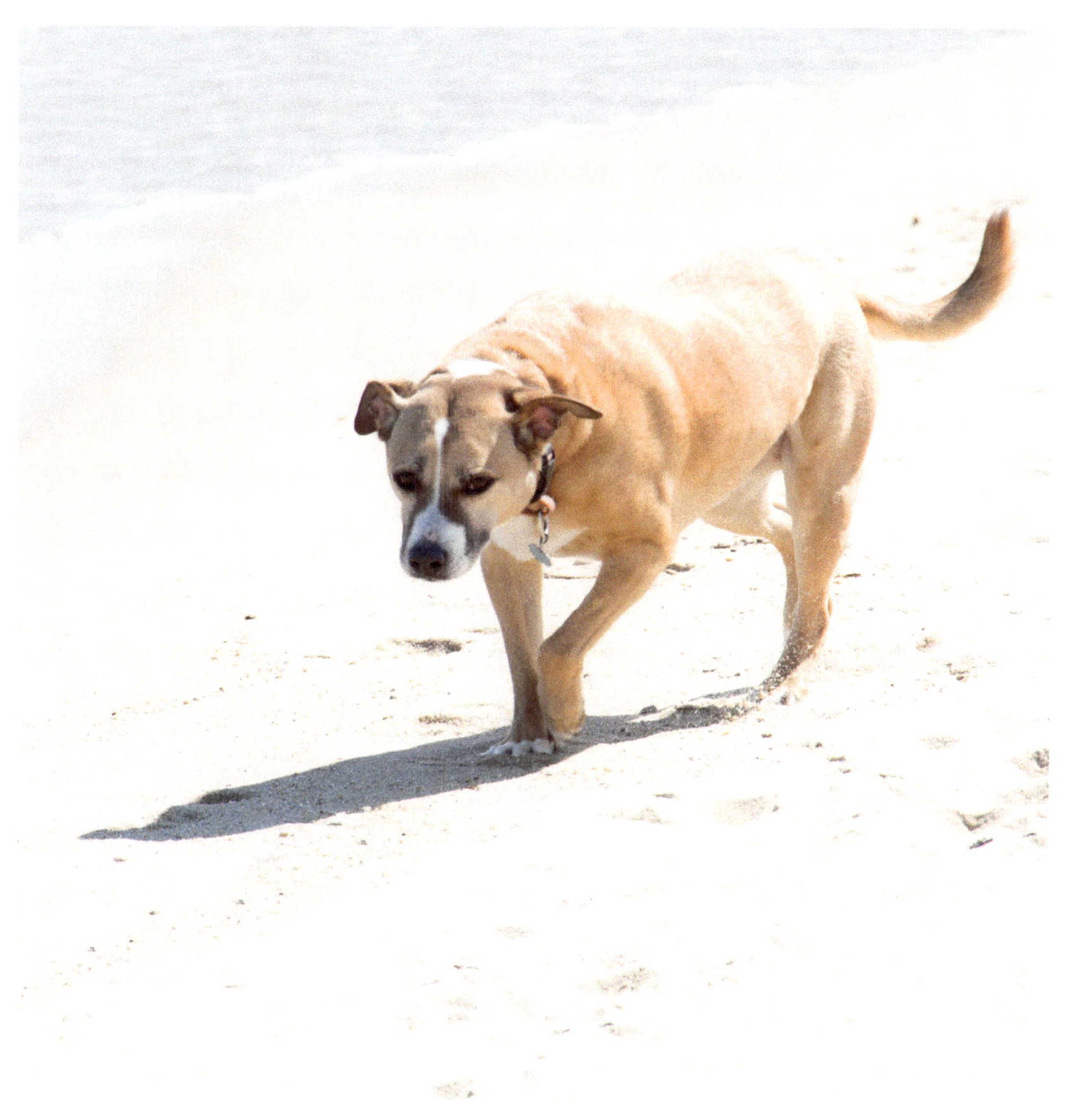

The Dogs of Plum Point

After a terrible heat yesterday
we wake early this morning
to discover a breeze.
We bring our cereal bowls outside
to eat at the picnic table
under the black walnut tree.
The dogs come with us.

Betsy comes from next door,
with her dog, Jesse, who is
blind and hard of hearing—
a little mop of dark grey curls
he follows the scent of our dogs,
our gentle pit bull Cooper,
our inherited sheep dog, Soda.

Betsy's friend, Rick, who lives
over in the Neeld Estate, comes up
from the beach with Isabel,
a bluetick hound with eyes
that seem too big for her head.
She looks up at me with a pitiful face.

Together the dogs fetch sticks,
chase rabbits in the tall grass,
drink from the same water bowl,
then fall asleep at our feet.
Except Jesse, who's too old for this romping.
He seeks out my air-conditioned porch.
He comes in with me to escape the heat,
curls up under the bench, keeps me
company while I write.

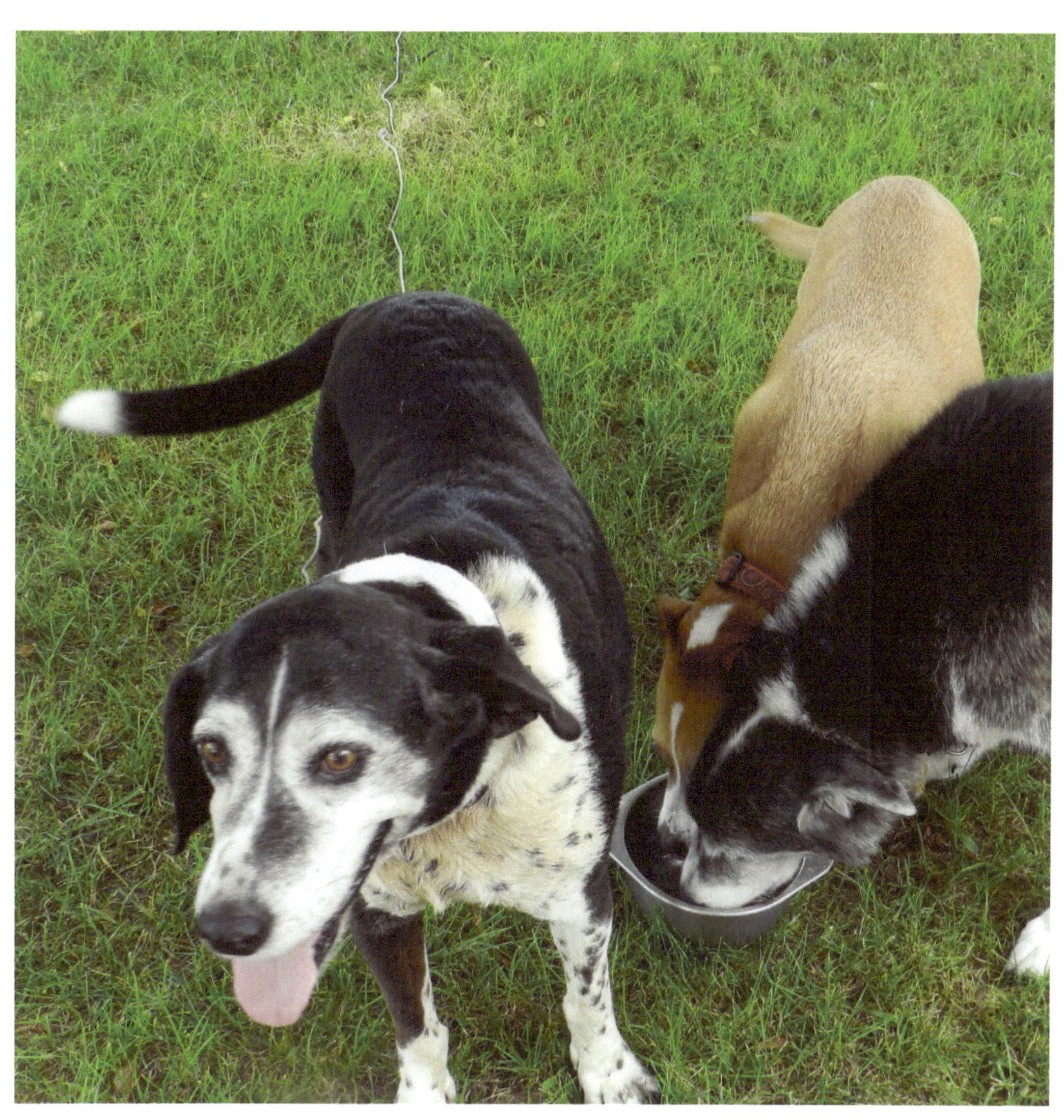

Cows in the Meadow

When I was a child,
my grandmother would sing to me:
Pigs in the clover,
cows in the meadow.

Now, I live with some
Black Angus cows—
four females, a steer and a calf—
a few hundred yards from the bay,
a few feet from my cottage door.
Mornings, I walk over
to visit them with my dog.

They poke their snouts through
the fence, curious as we are,
enjoying the scent
of other animals.
Everything is big
on their dark brown heads—
their eyes and their lashes,
their nostrils, their teeth.
Tails on a constant move
to keep the flies at bay.
Big soulful expressions seem
to ask, What's to become of us,
what's to become of our baby?

The landowner bought them
for a tax break, proof of a working farm.
The children come to feed them hay.
We all seem to know it's temporary.

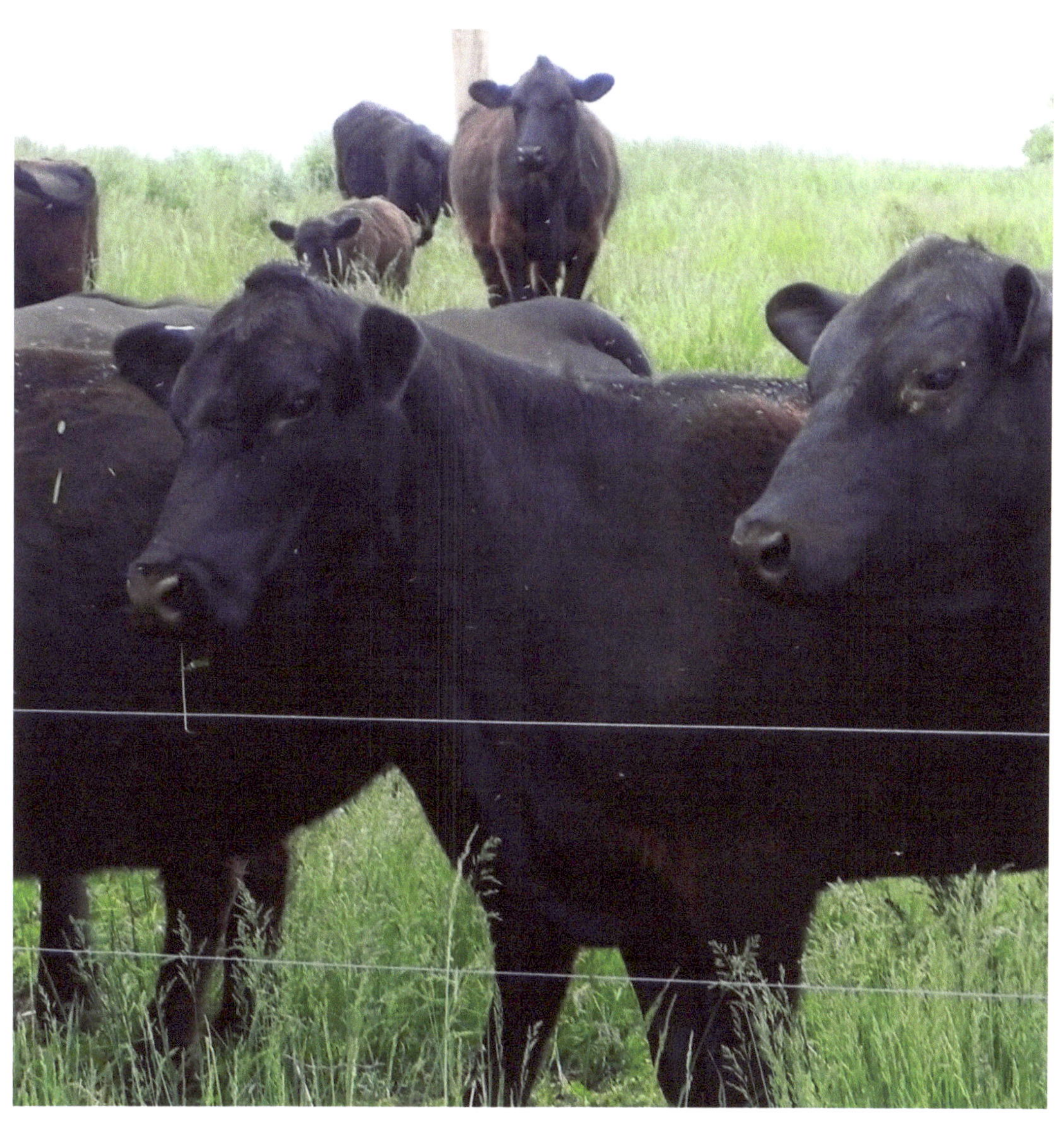

Sea Nettles

It takes a certain rise
in temperature and a certain
saltiness for them to appear,
so most likely they'll arrive in
time for fireworks on the Fourth
when the water's like a bathtub
and everyone's out barbequing.

And sure enough,
some small child will come
crying up the beach—stung.

Old wives tales say,
run for the vinegar, or
grab the meat tenderizer
left on the kitchen shelf
for just this reason.

An old fisherman
might say, "Just as well
to use your own pee."

Their umbrellas float
like small parachutes
beneath the surface.
Trailing red tenticles
defend their right to be here.
After all, we're just visiting.

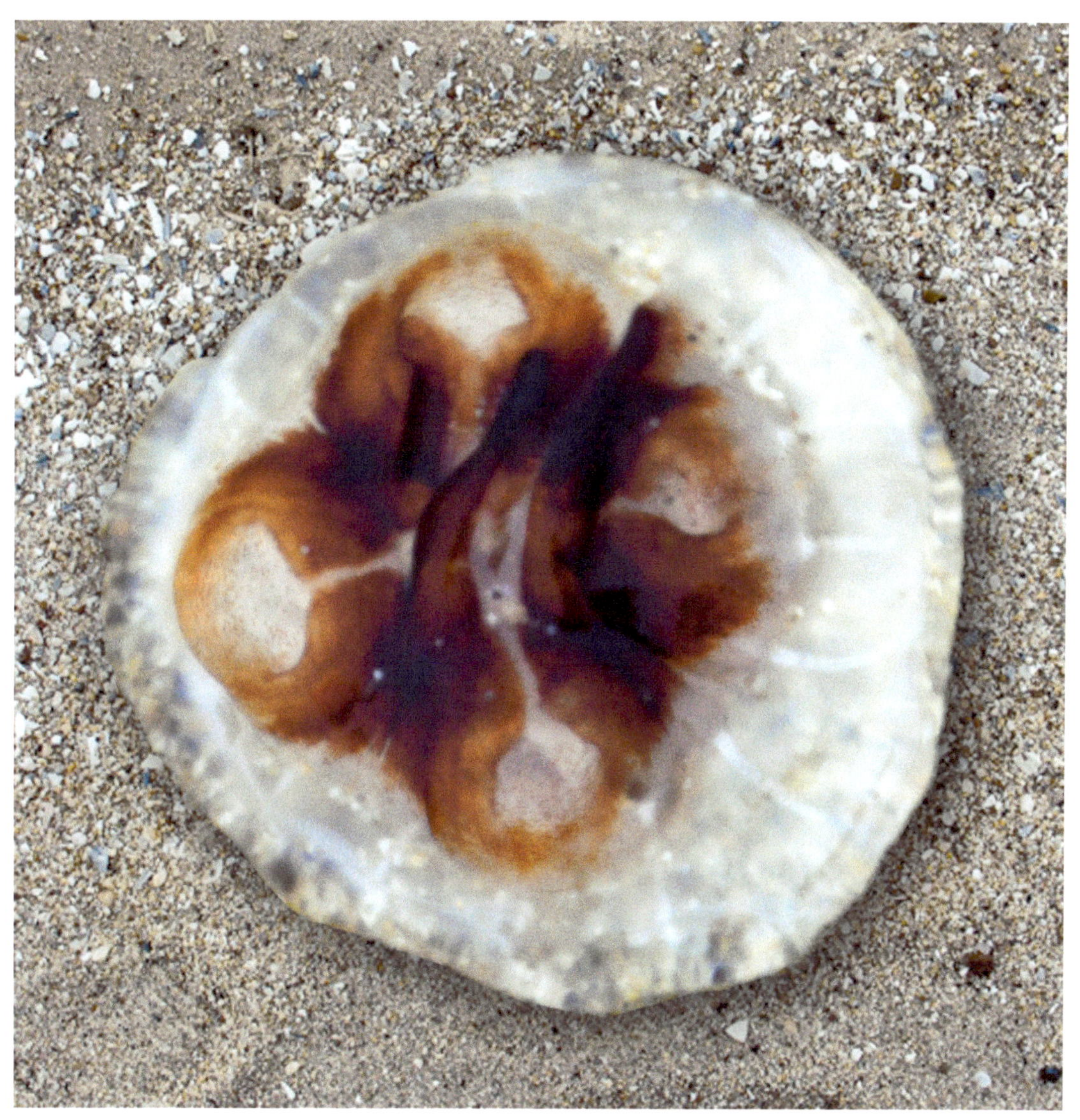

Summer Ceviche

Start with a big platter.

Slice the ripe avocado
you got from the grocery store
into crescents.

Grill the ears of corn.
Shave the slightly charred
kernels off each cob.

Add lima beans, and
the fresh nectarines
you bought at the open air market.

Drizzle everything
with olive oil and lime.

Set out the jelly jar glasses.
Uncork the wine.

Consider
what is to come—
the setting sun.

Light the outdoor
paper lanterns.

Announce: Dinner is served.
Allow yourself this happiness.

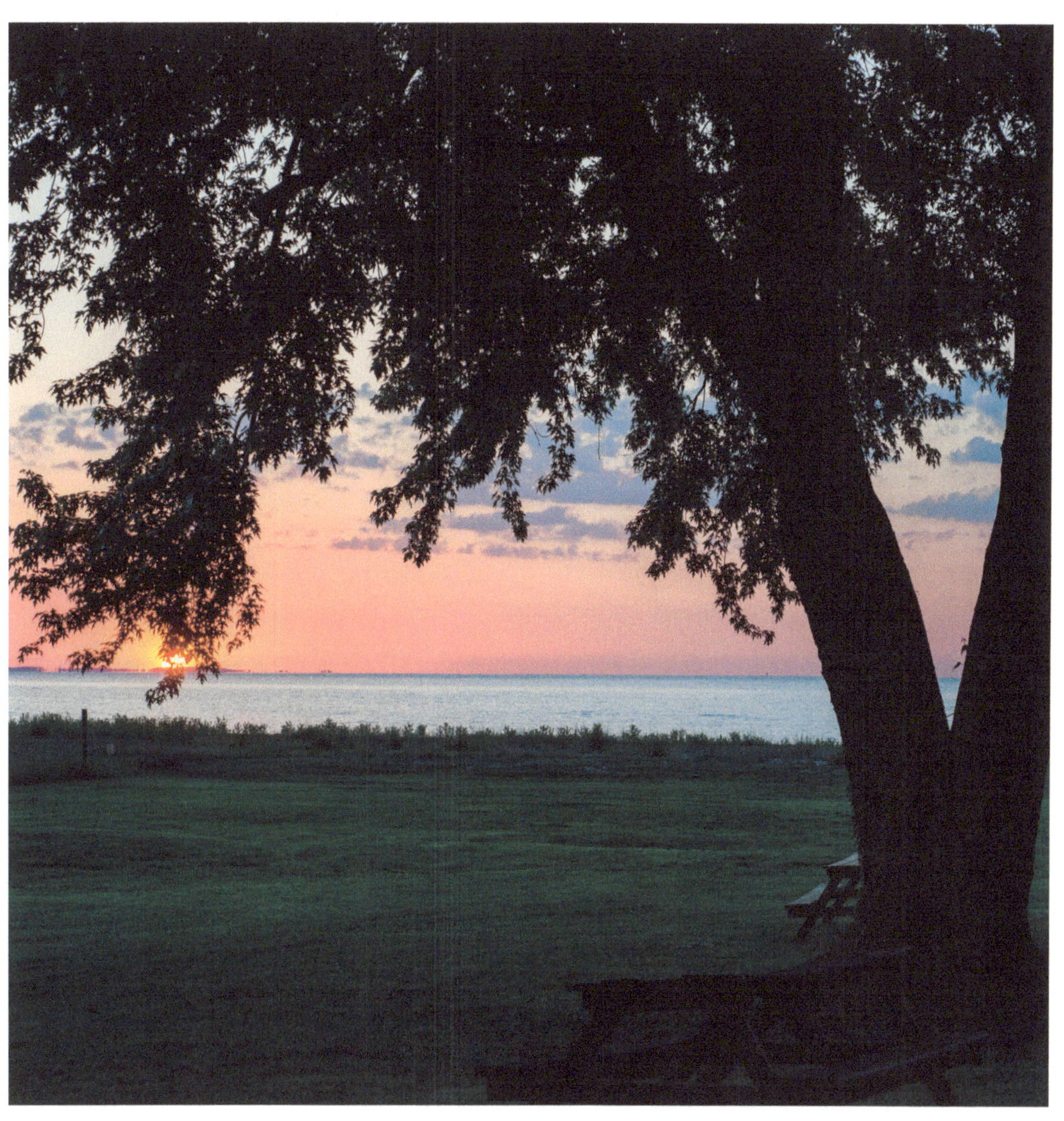

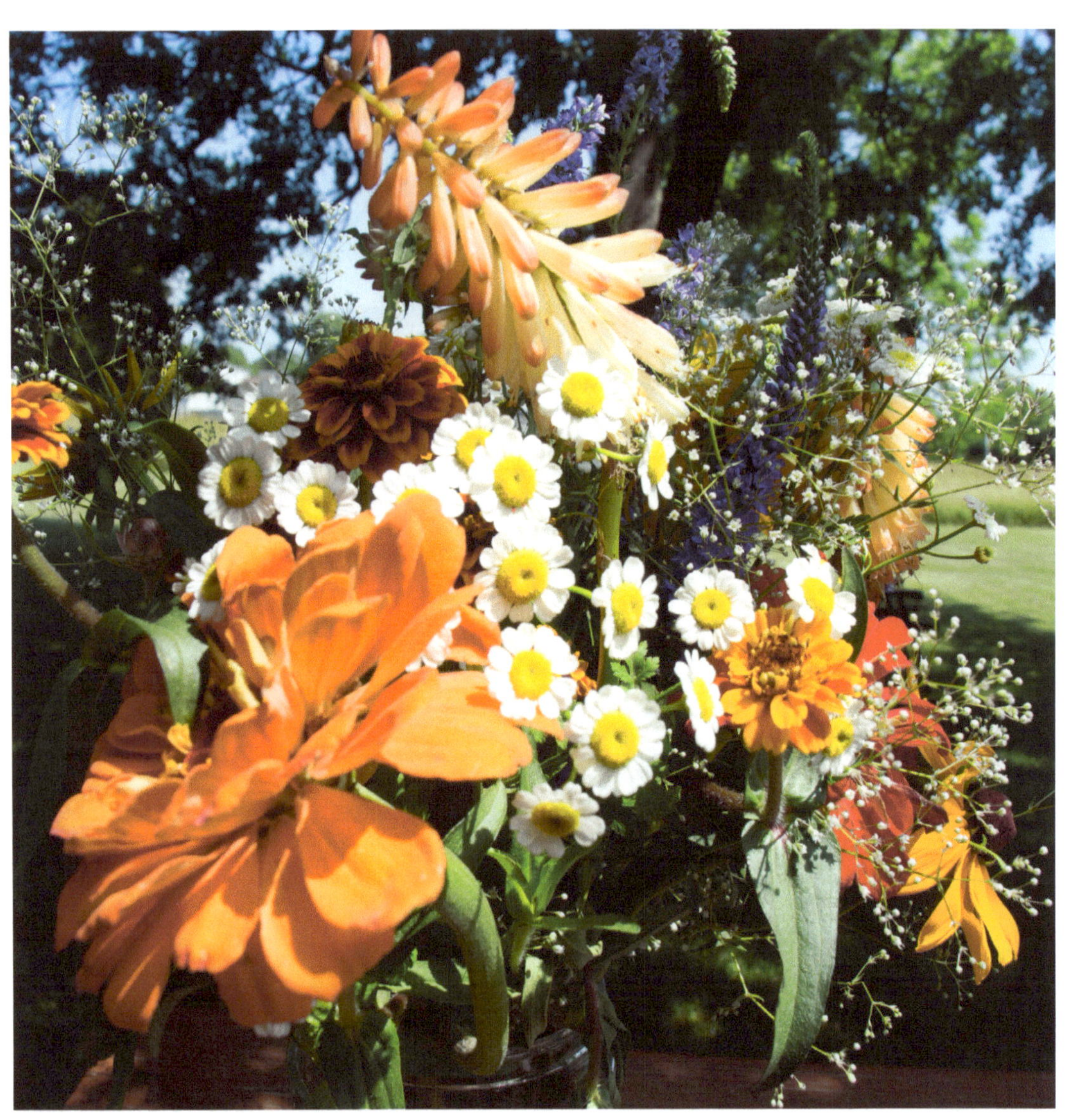

Evolution

Two summers ago
I made a homemade bee killer
to hang on the front porch—a funnel
filled with orange juice and liquid soap.
We couldn't sit out there—the bees would
hover around our Quince bush, crazy
for the coral flowers so strong in the light
they cast a blush on the patio floor.

The bees drank my concoction
and died from suffocation,
laying their double wings to rest.

Last summer, I read about
the bee's decline. In my regret,
I sought out flowers to attract bees:
cosmos, black eyed Susans, lupines.
Alas, I bought them cheap
at a home improvement store
where they'd been sprayed
with deadly pesticides.

This summer, I'm working on
a bee garden, planting desirous
pink and yellow snapdragons.
The bees know how to unlock
the flower and drink it's nectar.

I will make a bee house
from old wood,
and hang it in the shade.
I will make a safe place that sings:
O glorious bee.

En Plein Air

Before dawn Monet would set out
for the Normandy fields to paint
his first canvas of haystacks.
A half hour later, he would begin
again. Over time he painted
haystacks and hay bales
at different times of day,
from different angles,
in different seasons.

His assistant delivered the canvases
by wheelbarrow, a dozen or so
at a time, and Monet would
advance one depending on the light.
In winter the stacks appear violet and blue.
In summer they're fiery red and orange.

I too am out in the air, my picnic bench
a short distance from the hay field,
the sky above it a roll of canvas
that keeps revolving in blue and white.
A tractor arrives to cut and rake
the dry grasses. It rolls the hay
into coils that stand sentinel,
until the children come
to climb them and jump
like superheroes from a great height.

I don't have to go anywhere.
My field transforms before me
with the seasons, the time of day,
children coming and going.

At night the moon hangs
ever present, a light bulb
over the water.

Mornings, I begin again.

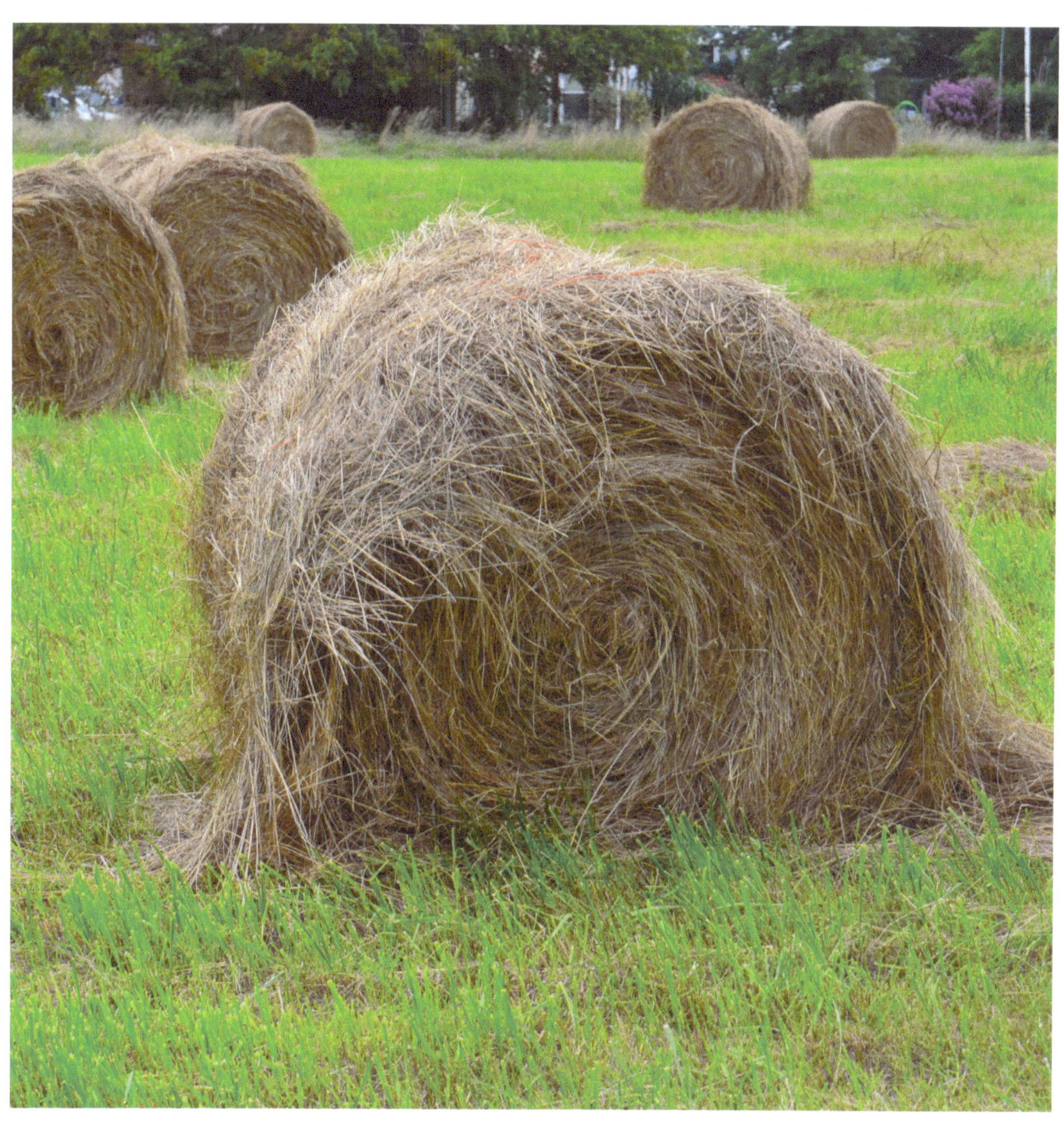

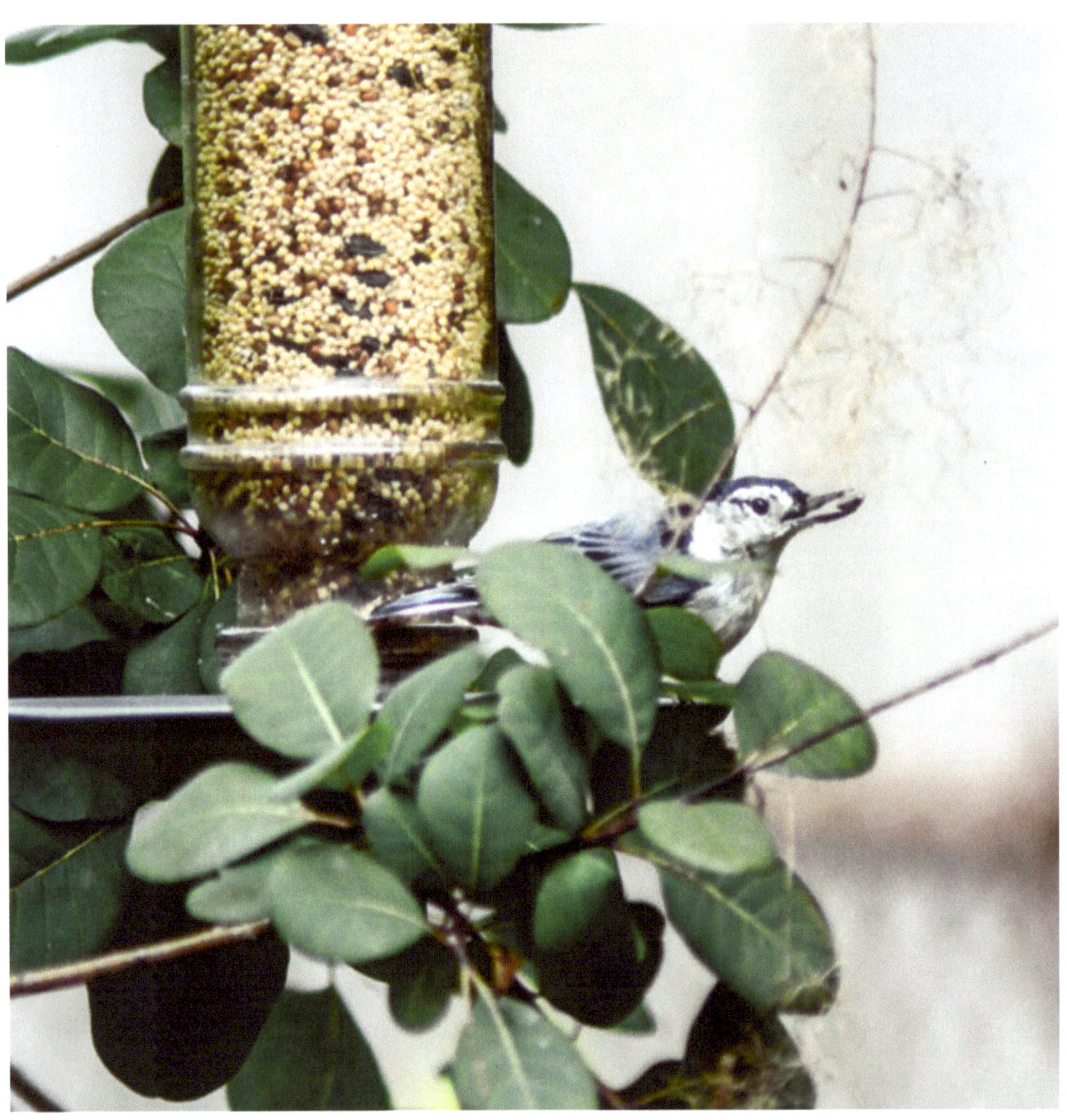

Grateful

for the birds of North America
who traverse my backyard—
the simple brown wrens,
the greyish bird with a white breast
and a stroke of white on his wings,
the smaller thing I can't identify,
moving too fast, a hummingbird perhaps.

Grateful for the singing,
the birds on the wire,
the gentle flyover to
the condominium bird feeder.

For the robins who always seem fatter
than the others,
the pair of cardinals, the showy male
in his dramatic black mask,
the retiring female's
soft brown feathers like dry dirt,
both with orange beaks.

Grateful for my chair,
the old aluminum one that rocks,
so I can watch the nest making.
A brown bird carries in his beak
a bit of dried tree fern.
You're welcome, take what you want.

Grateful for the years
and the gift of this yard,
grateful for the bird
that sings po-ta-to chip,
doves that coo and call out for love.

Grateful for my husband
who put up the feeders,
so there's traffic and song
all the day long.

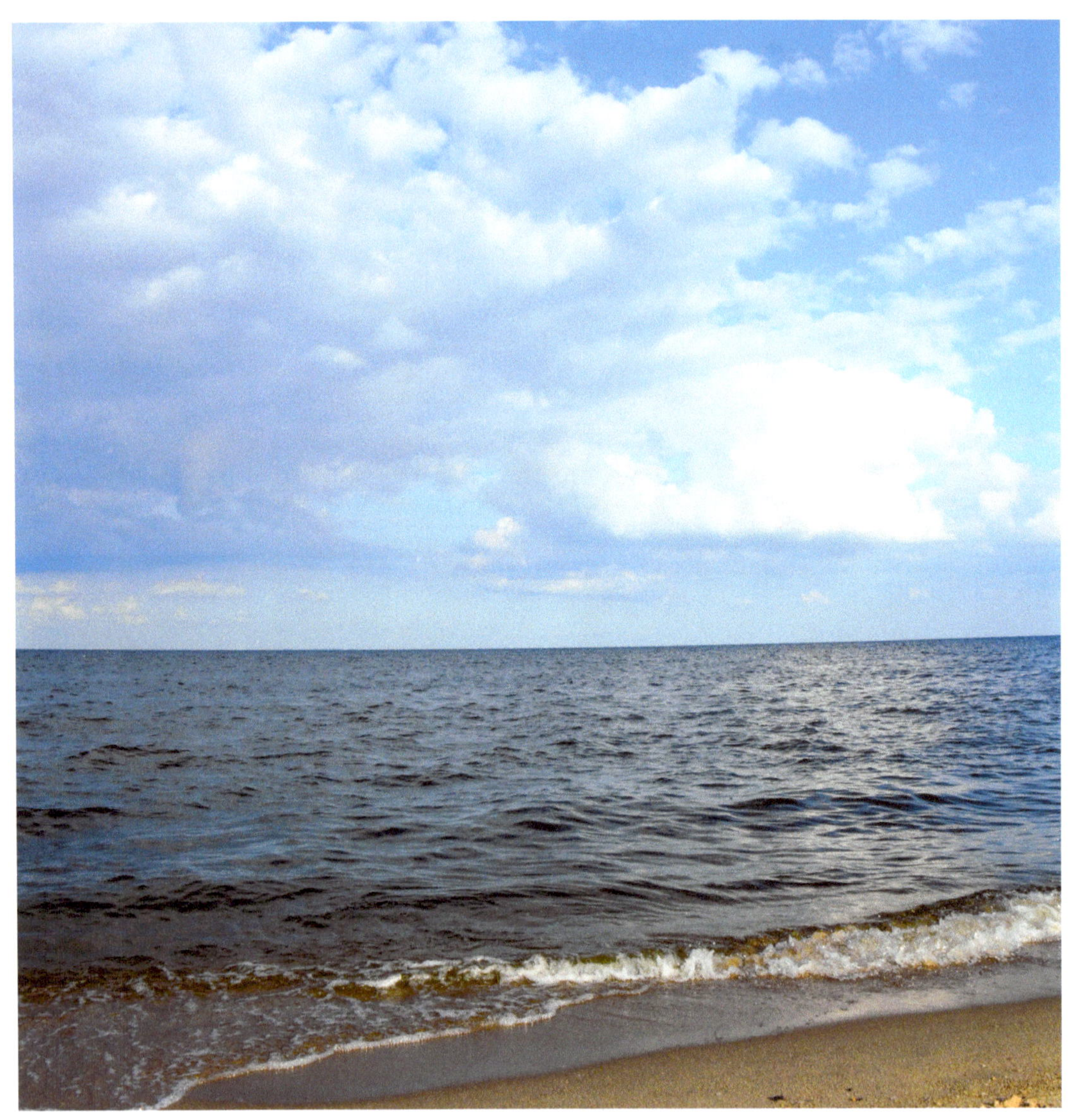

Plum Point, Late October

The grove of summer cottages,
abandoned for the winter.
Brown and yellow leaves
beginning to pile up.
Scattered bushes turning
orange, showing red berries.

Outdoor grills wobble
in the wind. Beach chairs
with seats of torn webbing
are left in the front yard.
Not sure these things will
survive the inevitable storms.

The rooster and roaming chickens
have gone home. The old man
won't be bothering us today.
My dog can walk without a leash.
He trots happily toward the cliffs
so I can look for fossils.

Now's the time to be here.
No need to speak to anyone.
No party revelers blaring their music.
No more luaus of roasted pig
and everyone drinking too much beer.
No more roaring jet skis.

The bay ripples.
Its color is quiet and faded,
a worn blue sweater.

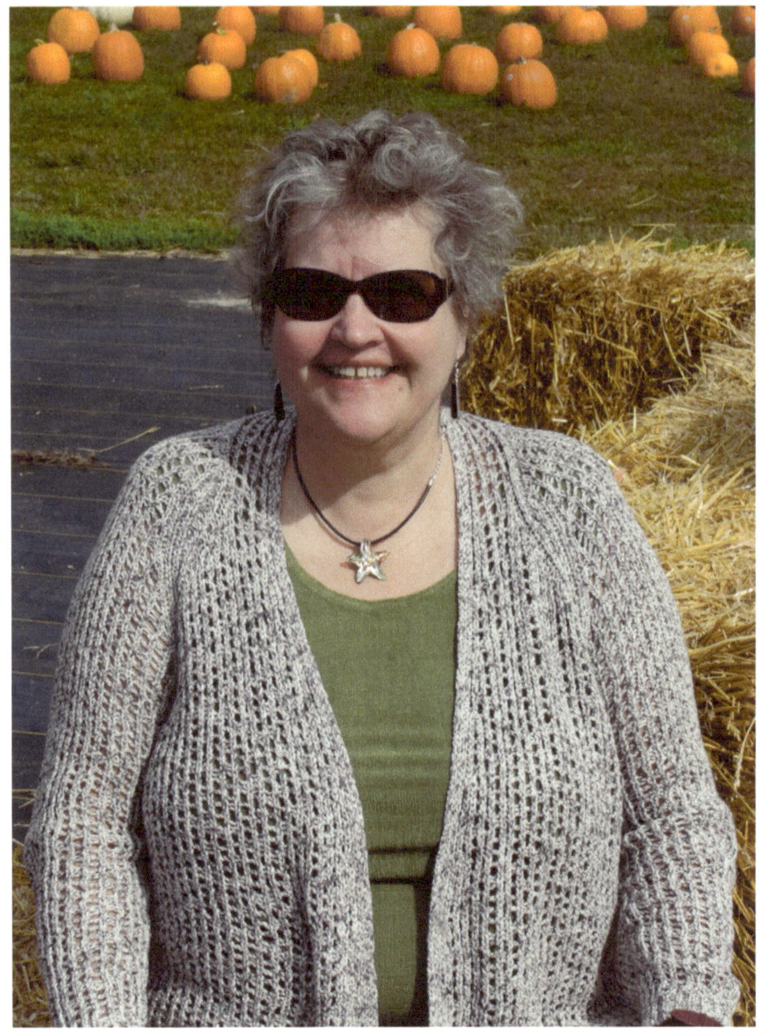

Christine Higgins — Author

Christine Higgins, poet and writer, is a recipient of a McDowell Colony fellowship and two Individual Artist Awards from The Maryland State Arts Council. Her work has appeared in many journals, including *Pequod, Little Patuxent Review, Lullwater Review, PMS (poemmemoirstory),* and *Poetry East.* Her chapbook, *Threshold,* was published in 2013 by Finishing Line Press. You can read additional work and learn more about her by visiting: www.christinehigginswriter.com.

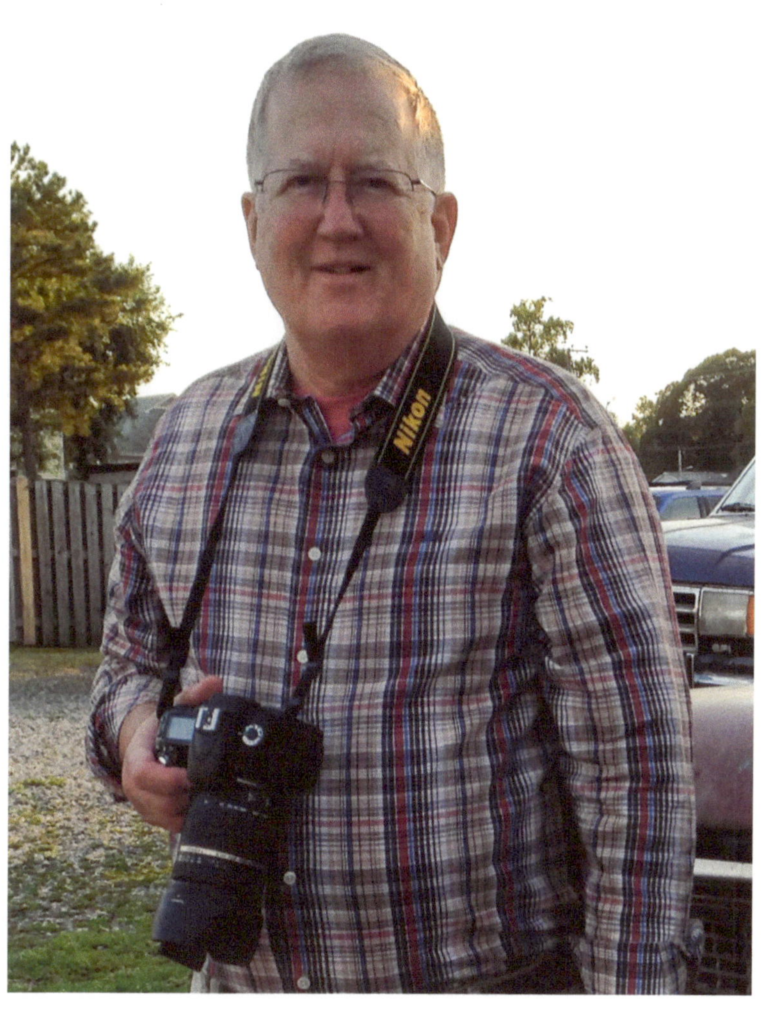

Kevin Higgins — Photographer

Kevin Higgins, a self-taught photographer, has been taking pictures ever since a cousin gave him his first camera when he was just a boy. Retired now from a long career, first as a Baltimore City Firefighter and then as an Agent for the Maryland Office of Parole and Probation, he has the opportunity to do what he loves best—venture out into the estuaries of the Chesapeake Bay to take photographs. You can see more of his photography by visiting his website: www.kevinhigginsphotography.com.

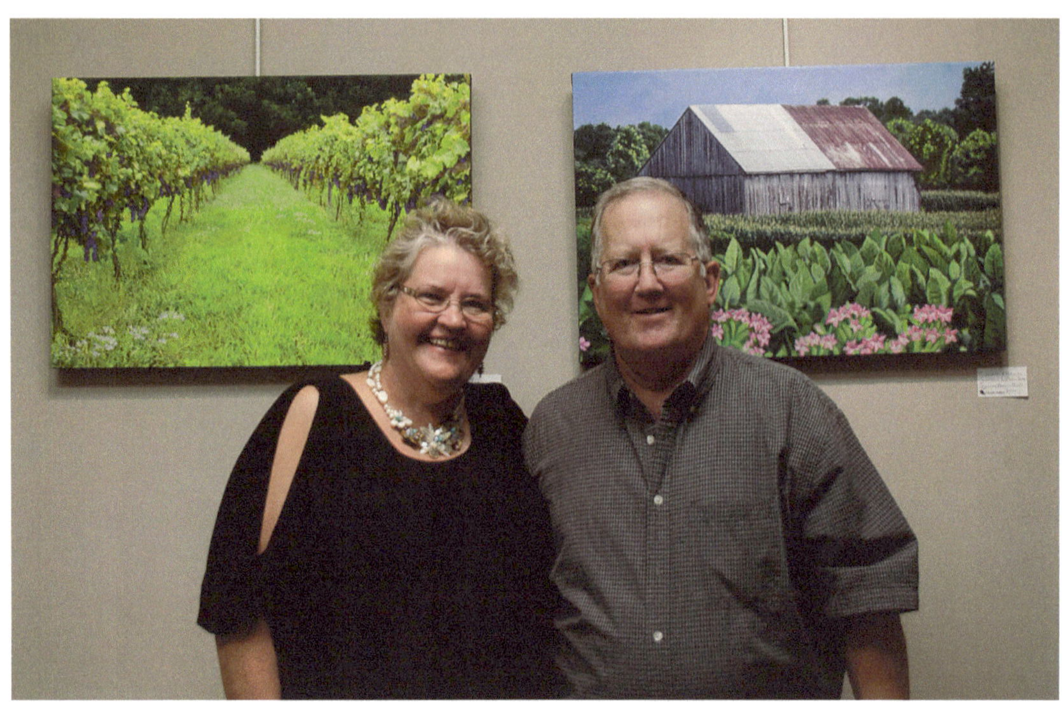

Acknowledgements

From the beginning, as we set out to create this collaborative book, we have felt supported in so many ways. We thank the Baker sisters, Deb and Chris, who so many years ago first shared with us their childhood vacation spot, Plum Point—what a gift it has been.

We thank the members of calvART Gallery in Prince Frederick, Maryland, who welcomed us with open arms and filled our lives with art and friendship.

We thank Suzanne Shelden, gifted painter and graphic designer, for her beautiful conception of our book and for always listening carefully.

Lastly, but always, we thank Christine's long-time writers' group—Ann LoLordo, Madeleine Mysko, and Kathleen O'Toole—who have been at the ready with good advice and loving support to both of us.